Luke: Artist and Theologian

Theological Inquiries

Studies in Contemporary
Biblical and Theological Problems

PAULIST PRESS
New York • Mahwah • Toronto

Luke: Artist and Theologian

Luke's Passion Account as Literature

Robert J. Karris, O.F.M.

PAULIST PRESS
New York • Mahwah • Toronto

Unless otherwise indicated, all biblical translations are based on the *Revised Standard Version*.

Library of Congress
Catalog Card Number: 84-61030

ISBN: 0-8091-2651-6

Published by Paulist Press
997 Macarthur Boulevard
Mahwah, N.J. 07430

Printed and bound in the
United States of America

CONTENTS

INTRODUCTION

This book is a study of Luke 23, Luke's passion account. As such, it deals with Luke's christology and soteriology. But it explores these two theological issues from a relatively unique viewpoint,[1] for I contend that Luke's artistry is a vehicle for his theology. Through a study of Luke's artistry I purpose to show that, although Luke places little or no stress on Jesus' death as an atonement for sin,[2] he does have a profound soteriological understanding of Jesus' death.

I explore Luke's artistry through a study of his major motifs/themes[3] of the faithful God,[4] justice, and food. Along the way of my analysis of the Gospel of Luke, especially Luke 23, I will touch on many of Luke's other themes: banquet, conversion, faith, fatherhood, grace, Jerusalem, joy, kingship, mercy, must, poverty, prayer, prophet, salvation, Spirit, temptation, today, universalism, way, and witness.[5] It is my contention that both the major and minor themes of Luke come together in Luke 23. This recapitulation of Luke's motifs forms a vast tapestry of meaning[6] as Luke declares thematically who Jesus is and how he saves.

In my first chapter I set forth my understandings of motif and of the nature of Luke Acts. In the next three chapters I probe the large question of how Jesus got himself crucified. I answer this question by pondering the motifs of justice and food. Jesus got himself crucified because his table fellowship with outcasts bodied forth an alien God and because his justice way of life was an intolerable challenge to the life-style of the religious leaders. In my fifth chapter I deal with Luke 23, with special emphasis on three points: Jesus' God who is endlessly faithful to him and communes with him in and through death; Jesus who as the suffering righteous one is faithful to God and is God's Son; Jesus who at the nadir of his power saves the ''good thief'' by granting him a place at the banquet of paradise. In a final chapter I gather together the strands of my argument.

As the number and the length of the notes alone will testify, this

1

book is meant to be scholarly. But it is not meant to be arcane and out of bounds for those who have a recent, basic course in New Testament under their belts.

This work has been in the pipeline for a number of years. It is with joy and gratitude that I acknowledge a generous grant from the Association of Theological Schools which made initial work on this project possible during a sabbatical leave in 1978–1979. I am deeply thankful for the intellectual stimulation I have received from members of the Luke-Acts study groups of the Catholic Biblical Association of America and the Society of Biblical Literature. Finally, as a token of gratitude to the school which has been and continues to be a godly influence on me in so many and varied ways, I dedicate this book to the pioneering presidents of Catholic Theological Union—Paul Bechtold, C.P. and Alcuin Coyle, O.F.M.

NOTES

1. This monograph is a modest contribution to the neglected area of the study of Luke's art. For a general orientation to this area of investigation, see W. C. van Unnik, "Eléments artistiques dans l'évangile de Luc," in *L'Evangile de Luc: Problèmes littéraires et théologiques: Memorial Lucien Cerfaux* (BETL 32; ed. F. Neirynck; Gembloux: Duculot, 1973) 129–40; Robert J. Karris, "Windows and Mirrors: Literary Criticism and Luke's Sitz im Leben," *Society of Biblical Literature 1979 Seminar Papers* (ed. Paul J. Achtemeier; SBLSPS 16; Missoula: Scholars, 1979) 1.47–58. Previous studies on Luke's artistry would include: Wilhelm Bruners, "Lukas—Literat und Theologe: Neue Literatur zur lukanischen Doppelwerk I–II," *Bibel und Kirche* 35 (1980) 110–12, 141–51; O. C. Edwards, Jr., *Luke's Story of Jesus* (Philadelphia: Fortress, 1981); Luke T. Johnson, *The Literary Function of Possessions in Luke-Acts* (SBLDS 39; Missoula: Scholars, 1977); Norman R. Petersen, *Literary Criticism for New Testament Critics* (Guides to Biblical Scholarship; Philadelphia: Fortress, 1978) 81–92; Charles H. Talbert, *Literary Patterns, Theological Themes, and the Genre of Luke-Acts* (SBLMS 20; Missoula: Scholars, 1974). For an excellent survey on recent research dealing with Luke-Acts, see Earl Richard, "Luke - Writer, Theologian, Historian: Research and Orientation of the 1970's," *BTB* 13 (1983) 3–15.

2. See I. Howard Marshall, *Luke: Historian and Theologian* (Grand Rapids: Eerdmans, 1971) 175: "The atoning significance of the death of Jesus is not altogether absent from Acts, but it is not the aspect which Luke has chosen to stress. His presentation of the saving work of Jesus is consequently one-

sided. . . . What is lacking is rather a full understanding of the significance of the cross as the means of salvation.''

3. Throughout this book I use theme and motif interchangeably. See chapter one below for more detail. The thematic approach I am pursuing in this work does not professedly try to ascertain what was going on behind the scenes in Luke's communities as he wrote Luke-Acts. Luke's themes, like that of Jesus' journey to the cross as a symbol of his fidelity to and love of the Father God, may address themselves to problems within Luke's communities, e.g., fidelity to the Christian Way during persecution. In this work I do not have the opportunity to relate theme to Sitz im Leben. On this relationship see the brief, but helpful remarks in William Freedman, "The Literary Motif: A Definition and Evaluation," *Novel* 4 (1970/71) 131. I am indebted to R. Alan Culpepper, "Mark 10:50: Why Mention the Garment?" *JBL* 101 (1982) 131–32 for the reference to Freedman's work. — For those interested in information about Luke's Sitz im Leben, see my "Missionary Communities: A New Paradigm for the Study of Luke-Acts," *CBQ* 41 (1979) 80–97; *Invitation to Luke* (Garden City: Doubleday Image, 1977) 13–22; *What Are They Saying About Luke and Acts? A Theology of The Faithful God* (New York: Paulist, 1979) 38–48. In brief, Luke, the pastoral theologian, is addressing situations of persecution, rich and poor, and continued mission to the Jews.

4. This work develops the initial insights of my earlier volume, *What Are They Saying About Luke and Acts?*, which bore the subtitle, *A Theology of The Faithful God*.

5. In 1970 John Navone published a volume with the title, *Themes of St. Luke* (Rome: Gregorian University Press). In it he treated the twenty themes, which I list here using his wording. His list could easily be expanded by adding, e.g., mighty deeds, seeing, and women. Navone did not interrelate the Lukan motifs nor did he relate them together in a study of Luke 23.

6. Or to use Paul Ricoeur's terminology, there is a deep "intersignification" within the various Lukan motifs. See his "Biblical Hermeneutics," *Semeia* 4 (1975) 100–06.

Chapter One

REFLECTIONS ON MOTIF AND LUKE'S GOSPEL[1] AS KERYGMATIC STORY OF THE FAITHFUL GOD

We all have an implicit notion of what a motif or theme is. In order that we might share a common and explicit understanding of motif, I begin with the definition of motif I will presuppose throughout this work.[2]

William Freedman defines motif in this way: "A motif, then, is a recurrent theme, character, or verbal pattern, but it may also be a family or associational cluster of literal or figurative references to a given class of concepts or objects. . . . It is generally symbolic—that is, it can be seen to carry a meaning beyond the literal one immediately apparent . . . ."[3]

Freedman also suggests that five basic factors determine the efficacy of a motif: (1) frequency; (2) avoidability and unlikelihood; (3) significance of the contexts in which it occurs; (4) the degree to which all instances of the motif are revelant to the principal end of the motif as a whole and to which they fit together into a recognizable and coherent unit; (5) appropriateness of the motif to what it symbolizes.[4]

Some examples from Luke's theme of food will illustrate these five basic factors. The theme of food occurs in every chapter of Luke's Gospel and therefore easily meets the criterion of frequency. A brief glance at the other Gospels shows that Luke could have avoided mention of Jesus at table in a number of instances, e.g., 11:37–54 which depicts Jesus eating with and castigating the religious leaders. The motif that God in Jesus provides food for a hungry creation occurs in all significant contexts in the Gospel of Luke: infancy narrative, Galilean ministry, jour-

5

ney to Jerusalem, last days in Jerusalem. The instances of the food motif
work together to fashion a powerful portrait of a God who cares for the
needy. Finally, the motif of food is very appropriate to what it symbolizes, God's renewed union with his estranged people.[5]

At this initial stage of our investigation of the Lukan themes, some
advice may be in order. The study of the Lukan motifs will draw us into
Luke's kerygmatic story in a deep way. As D. Robertson writes:

> The Bible's significance as literature is closely tied to the
> power of the literary symbolism present in its various books.
> The centripetal force of literary symbols draws the reader into
> the work, and, through an effort to unite its symbols in a total
> realization of its structure, one is led finally to surrender one-
> self to the force of the work.[6]

And as Paul Ricoeur reminds us, we will be giving voice to a mute
text: "The text is mute. An asymmetric relation obtains between text
and reader, in which only one of the partners speaks for the two. The text
is like a musical score and the reader like the orchestra conductor who
obeys the instructions of the notation."[7]

And it may even seem that once we have studied Luke's themes we
will have mastered his text and meaning and can excitedly call out to
colleagues and pew-frequenters, "I've got it! I know how Luke's theme
of justice fits together." But such excitement may be short-lived. For it
seems that like Dante in his *The Divine Comedy*, one of Luke's favorite
devices is to lure readers into thinking that they have captured the meaning of a theme only to find that it has eluded their conceptual grasp and
deals with something much more profound.[8] For example, Luke's justice theme deals with the reversal that the mighty will be put down from
their thrones and the lowly exalted (Luke 1:52) and finds resolution in
Luke 24's depiction of the exaltation of the lowly one par excellence, the
crucified Jesus. However, Luke 23–24 narrate that the mighty are not
really put down from their thrones, but offered forgiveness (23:34) by
the Jesus who lives out his teaching on love of enemies which he proclaimed in his sermon on the plain (6:27–28). Another example is found
in Luke's treatment of the religious leaders and the people. In most instances the religious leaders are stereotypically unjust and the people ea-
ger to respond to Jesus. In Luke 23 Joseph of Arimathea, a religious

leader and a member of the Sanhedrin, is just, and the people unjustly demand that Jesus be crucified. In pursuing Luke's theme of justice, readers may have their own views of justice and of a just God profoundly challenged.

In brief, a study of Lukan motifs will be richly rewarding, but it can be frustrating. The temptation will be constantly at the door to say that Luke is muddleheaded or inconsistent or not in control of his material.[9] The exploration of a Lukan theme is no Easter egg hunt. We, the pursuers, may become the pursued. As in the study of a rich tapestry, it will take time and the training of one's eyes and heart to appreciate the thematic interweaving of colors and patterns.

My role in our adventure of pursuing a Lukan motif is to be a guide. As a guide, I will sometimes show how a Lukan motif is expressed in the Greek language of the text. At times, too, I will bring relevant Old Testament and other ancient texts to bear on the meaning of the theme.[10] And I will consider my task happily discharged when you can delight in the Lukan themes of the faithful God, justice, and food, and explore, on your own, other Lukan themes like journey and women.[11]

LUKE'S GOSPEL AS KERYGMATIC STORY OF THE FAITHFUL GOD

In this section I will treat two points: (1) the nature of Luke's writing as indicated in the preface of Luke 1:1–4; (2) intimations in Luke 1:1–4 of the theme of the faithful God, which runs throughout the Gospel and finds a fullness of expression in Luke 23.[12]

LUKE'S GOSPEL IS A KERYGMATIC STORY

A thematic approach is very much in accord with the nature of Luke's literary classic. For the Gospel of Luke is a kerygmatic story[13] which employs themes to give certainty to its readers. A brief consideration of Luke 1:1–4 will support this contention. Luke's prologue reads as follows:

> [1]Inasmuch as many have undertaken to compose a narrative concerning the events which have been brought to fruition among us, [2]as those handed them on to us who were eye-wit-

nesses from the beginning and became servants of the word,
[3]it seemed opportune that I, too, having made an accurate investigation of all (the traditions) from the beginning, should
write an orderly account for your Excellency, Theophilus, [4]so
that you might come to appreciate the certainty of the instruction you have received.[14]

To call the Gospel of Luke a narrative, and a kerygmatic one at that, is
to make a provocative statement about its nature. It is not an historical
foundation for the kerygma as Hans Conzelmann has argued.[15] It is not
just "salvation history,"[16] although it certainly is that. It is not just didactic biography, although it has the element of paraenetic or exhortatory thrust in common with that genre of literature.[17] Rather the Gospel
of Luke is meant to preach to the reader in narrative form and to elicit
from the reader an act of Christian faith.[18] In the chapters that follow we
will have many opportunities to show the correctness of the position
which is stated here as we detect how the Lukan themes may deepen the
faith of Luke's readers. In sum, and perhaps stated too simply and almost self-evidently, Luke's narrative is Gospel proclamation/kerygma.

INTIMATIONS IN LUKE 1:1–4 OF THE THEME OF THE FAITHFUL GOD

In his prologue Luke introduces his readers to the theme of the
faithful God. It is intimated by the phrases: "which have been brought
to their fruition among us" (1:1); "an orderly account" (1:3); "so that
you might come to appreciate the certainty of the instruction you have
received" (1:4).

The phrase, "which have been brought to fruition among us"
(1:1), refers to Luke's promise and fulfillment scheme, which should
not be seen primarily as the fulfillment of so many Old Testament passages. What is involved in promise and fulfillment is God's fidelity to
himself and to his creation and people.[19] This phrase, along with the Lukan stress on God's plan or the divine necessity,[20] refers to the nature of
the righteous God who has acted against evil and for good in "the Christ
event."[21] It refers to the nature of the God who wants to be with people
and to fashion a universal people for himself ("among us"). It refers to
the nature of the God who continues to invite women and men to join

that people and who preserves that people from ultimate harm and for union with himself. Thus God's plan for the universe, as voiced in Luke's narrative of his dealings with his people, finds its fulfillment in Jesus' eating with sinners and outcasts, in the righteous Jesus' crucifixion and vindication, in the people gathered together through his Spirit, and will find its complete fulfillment when God will sit down and make merry with his creation at the eschatological banquet.[22] This God is the faithful God. And Luke's kerygmatic story, especially Luke 23, will use themes to urge his readers to a deeper faith in this God.

The phrase, "an orderly account" (1:3), points ahead to the order which Luke has used in fashioning his narrative. He has not constructed his narrative on the principle of chronological order. Rather his sequence of events is ordered according to the principle of how they relate to the plan and purpose of the faithful God. Thus before Luke narrates what Jesus does at Capernaum (4:31–41), he presents his programmatic account of Jesus fulfillment preaching at Nazareth (4:16–30). This "ordering" occasions chronological disharmony, for 4:23 refers to Jesus' works in Capernaum although Luke will not describe such until his account in 4:31–41. Luke is responsible for this sequence, which is disharmonious according to a chronological ordering. But in Luke's order the sequence is not strange. It fits into his order of showing programmatically, at the beginning of Jesus' public ministry, how God is faithful, in and through the ministry of Jesus the prophet, to his promises as set forth in Isaiah 61 and 58. Dillon puts this point well:

> Luke is conscious of the overarching and compelling logic of the divine plan at every step of his two-volume work, and the 'order' of each happening—where and when he locates it—expresses how it obeys that logic and fits that plan. . . . Summing up: Luke's 'orderly accounting' places all his raw materials in relationship to the totality of sacred history, as it came to completion in the Easter Christ.[23]

The final phrase is "so that you might come to appreciate the certainty of the instruction you have received" (1:4). The goal of the Lukan narrative is that the reader might come to faith, once again, on a deeper level. Through his themes Luke will invite and challenge his readers to a deeper assimilation of who God is and thus enable them to be more secure in their faith.[24] As Gerhard Schneider aptly expresses it: "Luke's order also makes *assurance* possible, once the reader is aware of Luke's thematic of promise and fulfillment. Partially fulfilled promises give assurance of greater fulfillment and of the definitive fulfillment of the history of salvation."[25] The God who was faithful to Jesus and brought about his fidelity will be faithful to those who believe and hope in him.

At this point in the inquiry the reader might object that the view being presented here of the faithful God puts Jesus Christ in a secondary position in Luke's Gospel. That objection surfaces an important consideration which will have to be dealt with in greater detail in our treatment of the christology of Luke 23. Suffice it to say here that the Gospel of Luke does deal with Jesus Christ, but does so through the perspective of who the God of Jesus Christ is. In our handling of the themes of Luke 23 we will catch glimpses of how the motif of the faithful God permeates the entire narrative. For example, the *prophet* Jesus, who is confident of God's care for him, speaks God's words of warning and forgiveness. Unbound, Jesus freely, courageously, and obediently goes on his *journey* to rendezvous with the God in whom he trusts and whom he calls Father. Jesus promises the "good thief" a place in paradise, but it is Jesus' faithful God who vindicates him, his *righteous and poor one*, by raising him from the dead.[26]

Luke's kerygmatic story will have achieved its purpose if readers deeply probed the Lukan themes, felt their faith stirred, and believed again in the God who was faithful to his righteous Son, Jesus, and promises to be faithful to all who trust and walk in his justice.[27]

NOTES

1. Because of constraints of space I will restrict my treatment primarily to the Gospel of Luke. Luke's second volume, the Acts of the Apostles, will be brought in from time to time. For an overall view of the thematic interrelationship between Luke's Gospel and Acts, see Charles H. Talbert, *Literary Patterns, Theological Themes and the Genre of Luke-Acts.*

2. Many Lukan studies employ theme and motif interchangeably. See e.g., Navone, *Themes of St. Luke* and Arthur Vööbus, *The Prelude to the Lukan Passion Narrative: Tradition-, Redaction-, Cult-, Motif-Historical and Source-Critical Studies* (Papers of the Estonian Theological Society in Exile, Scholarly Series 17; Stockholm: Estonian Theological Society in Exile, 1968). For sim-

plicity's sake, throughout this study I will follow the common Lukan scholarly parlance and use theme and motif interchangeably.

3. "The Literary Motif," 127–28.

4. Ibid., 126–27.

5. As the above formulations of the motif of food indicate, a motif cannot be expressed in a single declarative sentence. It is multifaceted. One must continue to look at the motif from new and various angles in order to begin to comprehend its richness. My attempts to formulate the riches of the Lukan motif of food do not include, among other elements, hospitality and eating with unclean people.

6. "Literature, the Bible as," *IDBSup* 549.

7. *Interpretation Theory: Discourse and the Surplus of Meaning* (Fort Worth: Texas Christian University Press, 1976) 75.

8. I owe this insight to one of my students, Daria L. Donnelly. See further and more technically, Wolfgang Iser, *The Implied Reader: Patterns of Communication in Prose Fiction from Bunyan to Beckett* (Baltimore: Johns Hopkins, 1974) 282–90.

9. The model of "organic unity" will not do justice to a study of Luke's themes. Luke argues narratively more by juxtaposition of themes. See my "Windows and Mirrors," 55. For a different perspective, see Eduard Schweizer, *Luke: A Challenge to Present Theology* (Atlanta: John Knox, 1982).

10. I mention these aspects of my guidance to give an advance answer to those who may ask whether my thematic studies might be importing alien understandings into the Lukan text, e.g., those of contemporary English literature and of liberation theology. Our study of the Lukan motifs is firmly grounded in the Lukan text itself via crossreferencing to other instances of the particular Lukan motif under consideration and via examinations of the meanings of the Greek words which Luke employs. In addition, we consider the Old Testament as the major thematic forerunner to the Lukan themes and are methodologically loath to import contemporary understandings of words and themes into our appreciation of Luke. Furthermore, we have the imprimatur of premiere scholars like W.C. van Unnik, "Eléments artistiques," that Luke's artistry has many parallels in works by authors contemporary with Luke. See, for instance, what van Unnik, ibid., 137–38, has to say about the *drama* of Luke's passion account. —Let me give two advance samplings of my guidance. In our investigation of the meaning of the Greek word, *dikaios*, in Luke 23:47, we will say that it probably means both "innocent" and "righteous." In its meaning of "righteous," this word fits into the larger Lukan motif of "justice," which runs throughout the Gospel and is introduced already in Luke 1:6. I take another sampling, this time from the Lukan motif of food. An investigation of the Pharisees, the covenanters at Qumran, and Graeco-Roman friendship styles will reveal that

all these folks ate with people whom they considered their equals and whom they considered to be clean. In contrast, the Lukan Jesus eats with sinners and other unclean people. In brief, we explore the Lukan motifs in their literary, theological, cultural, and historical contexts.

11. See Freedman, "The Literary Motif," 131 on how pursuit of a theme enhances literary enjoyment of a text. In the course of my argument I will provide brief and select bibliographies on the various Lukan motifs, so that interested readers may explore them at their leisure.

12. I will contend below that the theme of the faithful God is the Lukan master theme which is played out in different ways by the themes of Jesus as prophet, Jesus as righteous one, justice, and food.

13. For the term "kerygmatic story," I am gratefully dependent upon Jack Dean Kingsbury, *Jesus Christ in Matthew, Mark, and Luke* (Proclamation Commentaries; Philadelphia: Fortress, 1981) 96 and passim.

14. Richard J. Dillon provides a verse-by-verse exegesis justifying this translation of his in "Previewing Luke's Project from His Prologue (Luke 1:1–4)," *CBQ* (1981) 205–27.

15. A convincing case against Conzelmann's interpretation (*The Theology of St Luke* [London: Faber and Faber, 1960]) has been made by Dillon, "Prologue," 208–09. See also Richard, "Luke," 3–5.

16. It is not my intention to rehearse the vast literature and discussion about the historical reliability of Luke-Acts. In this connection what is important is that Luke sets his narrative in the context of what the God of creation and of Israel has done in the past. Luke-Acts is a narrative celebration of what the God, confessed in the Old Testament, has done for creation and humankind in Jesus Christ. See C.K. Barrett: " . . . what we must observe is that they (the Old Testament writers) wrote history as a confession of faith" (*Luke the Historian in Recent Study* [Facet Books, Biblical Series 24; Philadelphia: Fortress, 1970]) 18.

17. It is the opinion of Charles H. Talbert that Luke-Acts is a type of didactic biography. See his *Literary Patterns, Theological Themes and the Genre of Luke-Acts*; see also his *What Is a Gospel? The Genre of the Canonical Gospels* (Philadelphia: Fortress, 1977) and "Biographies of Philosophers and Rulers as Instruments of Religious Propaganda in Mediterranean Antiquity," in *Augstieg und Niedergang der roemischen Welt: Geschichte und Kultur Roms in Spiegel der neueren Forschung* (Berlin: Walter de Gruyter, 1978), 2/16/ 2.1619–51. For a persuasive and substantial critique of Talbert's position, see D.E. Aune, "The Problem of the Genre of the Gospels: A Critique of C.H. Talbert's What is a Gospel?" in *Gospel Perspectives: Studies of History and Tradition in the Four Gospels* (ed. R.T. France; David Wenham; Sheffield: JSOT Press, 1981), 2.9–60. While Talbert's position may not carry conviction, he has pointed the attention of scholars to two very important dimensions in Luke's

Gospel. First, much of what Luke has written is of paraenetic or exhortatory value, e.g., Jesus at prayer, Jesus who forgives those responsible for his crucifixion. In this respect Luke's Gospel is didactic. Secondly, Talbert has detected that dimension in Luke's writing which makes it more readily understandable in another culture. The traces of didactic biography in Luke's Gospel would appeal to a Graeco-Roman, non-Semitic interested reader who would be familiar with this type of writing. On this latter point see Talbert's excellent study: *The Certainty of the Gospel: The Perspective of Luke-Acts* (DeLand: Stetson University Press, 1980); and see now his *Reading Luke: A Literary and Theological Commentary on the Third Gospel* (New York: Crossroad, 1982).

18. On this point, see Kingsbury, *Jesus Christ* 96 and passim. See also Joseph A. Fitzmyer, *The Gospel According to Luke (I–IX): Introduction, Translation, and Notes* (AB 28; Garden City: Doubleday, 1981) 145–62, e.g., 152: "It is difficult to imagine that Luke's purpose did not include an accosting of reader Theophilus and an eliciting from him of an act of Christian faith." See further the thesis of Richard Gloeckner, *Die Verkuendigung des Heils beim Evangelisten Lukas* (Walberberger Studien, Theologische Reihe 9; Mainz: Gruenewald, n.d. [1976]).

19. Significant studies on Luke's use of the promise and fulfillment motif would include the following. Paul Schubert insightfully highlighted the Lukan master concern that God's action in Jesus was part of his plan. He called this concern "proof from prophecy." See his "The Structure and Significance of Luke 24," in *Neutestamentliche Studien fuer Rudolf Bultmann zu seinem siebzigsten Geburtstag am 20. August 1954* (BZNW 21; Berlin: Toepelmann, 1954) 165–86. See now from a different perspective, Charles H. Talbert, "Prophecies of Future Greatness: The Contribution of Greco-Roman Biographies to an Understanding of Luke 1:5–4:15," in *The Divine Helmsman: Studies on God's Control of Human Events Presented to Lou H. Silberman* (ed. James L. Crenshaw; Samuel Sandmel; New York: Ktav, 1980) 129–41. In a superb study Paul S. Minear recast Schubert's insight into the framework of promise and fulfillment: "Luke's Use of the Birth Stories," in *Studies in Luke-Acts: Essays Presented in Honor of Paul Schubert* (ed. Leander E. Keck; J. Louis Martyn; Nashville: Abingdon, 1966) 111–30. Minear's article is also an excellent critique of Conzelmann's *Theology of St Luke*. On "promise and fulfillment" as the basic category of biblical eschatology, see Nils A. Dahl, *The Crucified Messiah and Other Essays* (Minneapolis: Augsburg, 1974) 144: "What forms the central theme of biblical eschatology is not so much the end of the world and of history as the fulfillment of God's promises. For the New Testament, Jesus Christ is an eschatological figure, and the events connected with his name are eschatological principally because through him the promises of God are fulfilled." On the Christian and Jewish interpretations of scriptural fulfillment at the time

of Luke, see the perceptive work by David L. Tiede, *Prophecy and History in Luke-Acts* (Philadelphia: Fortress, 1980). See further James A. Sanders, "Isaiah in Luke," *Int* 36 (1982) 144–55.

20. On this Lukan theme, see Fitzmyer, *Luke* 179–81.

21. In what follows "the events of Jesus' life, death, resurrection, ascension, and sending of the Spirit" will be referred to by the rubric, "the Christ event."

22. For the ideas expressed in this paragraph I am indebted to Richard J. Dillon, *From Eye-Witnesses to Ministers of the Word: Tradition and Composition in Luke 24* (AnBib 82; Rome: Biblical Institute, 1978) 205, 287 n. 155 and passim; James D.G. Dunn, *Christology in the Making: A New Testament Inquiry Into the Origins of the Doctrine of the Incarnation* (Philadelphia: Westminster, 1980) 234–35; William S. Kurz, "Luke-Acts and Historiography in the Greek Bible," *Society of Biblical Literature 1980 Seminar Papers* (ed. Paul J. Achtemeier; SBLSPS 19; Chico: Scholars, 1980) 283–300. See also Sanders, "Isaiah in Luke," 155: "God is both committed to his promises and free to surprise and even re-create us." It will be argued in the chapters that follow that the Christ event is the supreme articulation of God's promises for creation, of his fidelity to himself, to his creation and to humankind. These purposes have yet to be fulfilled totally, and thus Luke-Acts is open-ended, but open-ended toward the future in a most hopeful way because of what God has revealed about himself in the Christ event.

23. "Prologue," 223.

24. See Paul S. Minear, "Dear Theo: The Kerygmatic Intention and Claim of the Book of Acts," *Int* 27 (1973) 131–50, esp. 135–40.

25. *Das Evangelium nach Lukas: Kapitel 1–10* (Okumenischer Taschenbuchkommentar zum Neuen Testament 3/1; Guetersloh: G. Mohn/Wuerzburg: Echter, 1977) 41. See also Dillon, "Prologue," 226–27: "What gospel-narrative did was lay out faith's object more fully and circumstantially, showing that the words of promise and the events did in fact coincide, but leaving it faith's business to decide, albeit more 'securely': it is God who worked this sequence of promise and fulfillment, and he worked it for my salvation!"

26. The interested reader might want to consult the opening of Luke's story, Luke 1:5–2:52, to see how often those verses refer to God as the agent of the action in the story. A modest count is forty times.

27. See Roland M. Frye, "The Jesus of the Gospels: Approaches Through Narrative Structure," in *From Faith to Faith: Essays in Honor of Donald G. Miller on His Seventieth Birthday* (ed. Dikran Y. Hadidian; Pittsburgh Theological Monograph Series 31; Pittsburgh: Pickwick, 1979) 77: "The evangelists were not attempting to record a chronicle of events in accurate chronological sequence, but were intent upon recreating structures of experience into which we

are invited to enter; they should be understood as narrators who construct a literary universe of experience and value, who bring us into contact with the living personality of Jesus, and who involve us in the declaration of a response to his message.''

Chapter Two

HOW DID JESUS
GET TO THE CROSS?
A PRELIMINARY ANSWER

Before taking a detailed look at Luke 23, we will address ourselves to a fundamental question which lies behind that chapter: In Luke's kerygmatic narrative how did Jesus get himself crucified? An initial answer is: Jesus got to the cross by being God's righteous person and by being the prophet of God's good news to the poor.[1]

JESUS AS GOD'S RIGHTEOUS ONE

The common Lukan way of referring to Jesus as the righteous one (see Luke 23:47; Acts 3:14; 7:52; 22:14) may not be familiar to the reader. The righteous person is the one who does God's will. And to say that Jesus is the righteous one is to proclaim that "he is the doer of God's will in the fullest sense."[2] But as doers and consequently living embodiments of God's will, righteous persons are subject to persecution by those whose non-righteous life-style is challenged by their righteous way of life. The persecuted person becomes a double test-case: (1) for the integrity of the one being persecuted: will she/he endure such torment without moral collapse? (2) for God's fidelity: will God rescue this faithful doer of his will? Is God faithful? Does God really care, not only for this persecuted one, but in this person for all his creation whose goodness seems to be constantly disfigured by evil?

One of Luke's ways of explaining how Jesus got to rendezvous with the cross and the power of darkness (22:53) is this thematic of the "suffering righteous one." In anticipation I point the reader's attention ahead to Luke 23:34b,35,36,46 where Luke uses three psalms of the innocently suffering righteous one (Psalms 22,29,31) to interpret Jesus' crucifixion. The reader should also note Luke 23:47, a prime Lukan verse for explaining Jesus' life and death. The centurion's confession of faith in Luke 23:47 is not the Markan "Truly this man was the Son of God" (15:39). Rather it is "Certainly this man was righteous."[3]

Wisdom 2:10-20 and 4:20-5:8 are excellent examples of the theme of the "righteous person."[4] In my quotation of this example I will italicize significant words and phrases and provide the Greek original for other key words and phrases. In subsequent discussions cross-references will be made to this vital example.

Wisdom 2:10-20

[10]Let us oppress *the righteous poor man (penēta dikaion)*; let us not spare the widow nor regard the gray hairs of the aged. [11]But let our might be our law of *right (dikaiosynēs)*, for what is weak proves itself to be useless. [12]Let us lie in wait for *the righteous man*, because he is inconvenient to us and opposes our actions; he reproaches us for sins against the law, and accuses us of sins against our training. [13]He professes to have knowledge of God, and calls himself *a child of the Lord*. [14]He became to us a reproof of our thoughts; [15]the very sight of him is a burden to us, because *his manner of life is unlike that of others*, and his ways are strange. [16]We are considered by him as something base, and he avoids our ways as unclean; he calls the last end of *the righteous* happy, and boasts that *God is his father*. [17]Let us see if his words are true, and let us test what will happen at the end of his life; [18]for if *the righteous man is God's son*, he will help him, and will deliver him from the hand of his adversaries. [19]Let us test him with insult and torture, that we may find out how gentle he is, and make trial of his forbearance. [20]Let us condemn him to a shameful death, for, according to what he says, he will be protected.

Wisdom 4:20-5:8

[20]They will come with dread when their sins are reckoned up, and their lawless deeds will convict them to their face. [1]Then *the righteous man* will stand with great confidence in the pres-

ence of those who have afflicted him, and those who make light of his labors. ²When they see him, they will be shaken with dreadful fear, and they will be amazed at his unexpected salvation. ³They will speak to one another in repentance, and in anguish of spirit they will groan, and say, This is the man whom we once held in derision and made a byword of reproach—we fools! We thought that his life was madness and that his end was without honor. ⁵Why has he been numbered among *the sons of God*? And why is his lot among the saints? ⁶So it was we who strayed from the way of truth, and the light of *righteousness* did not shine on us. ⁷We took our fill of the paths of *lawlessness* and destruction, and we journeyed through trackless deserts, but the way of the Lord we have not known. ⁸What has our *arrogance* (*hyperēphania*) profited us? And what good has our boasted *wealth* (*ploutos*) brought us?

JESUS AS GOD'S REJECTED PROPHET

By being God's righteous person, whose way of life was offensive to others, Jesus met with opposition and the cross. But the theme of God's persecuted righteous one is not sufficient for Luke's purposes of telling his kerygmatic narrative.[5] He also employs the thematic of God's "rejected prophet." A mere glance at some passages will indicate the centrality of "Jesus as God's prophet" in Luke's Gospel.

At the very beginning of his public ministry Jesus reveals his prophetic nature as one possessed by God's Spirit to proclaim good news to the poor and therefore as the fulfillment of God's promises made to Isaiah (see Luke 4:18,24). Witnesses to Jesus' mighty deed of raising the only son of the widow of Nain say of Jesus, "A great prophet has arisen among us!" and "God has visited his people!" (7:16). Three times the prophet Jesus predicts the salvific events of his passion and vindication (9:22–23; 9:43b–45; 18:31–34). Jesus walks the ways of the prophets, goes to Jerusalem like them, and will be killed there as they were (13:33–34).

In the context of Luke 23 and within that chapter itself there are a number of references to Jesus as prophet. By casting out the sellers in the temple, Jesus performs a prophetic action of God's cleansing of his temple of injustices (19:45–46). People mock Jesus by striking the blindfolded prophet Jesus and commanding him, "Prophesy! Who is it that struck you?'' (22:64). In 23:28–30 Jesus pronounces a prophetic warning to the women who mourn for him, and then asks for forgiveness for his enemies (23:34). To the ''good malefactor'' Jesus predicts that he will be with him in Paradise ''today'' (23:43). The two disciples on the way to Emmaus talk about Jesus of Nazareth, ''who was a prophet mighty in deed and word before God and all the people, and how our chief priests and rulers delivered him up to be condemned to death, and crucified him'' (24:19–20).[6]

That Jesus is a prophet is important in Luke's Gospel. But this theme is only comprehended fully when it is seen from the vantage point of Jesus as God's ''rejected prophet.'' The pattern of the ''rejected prophet'' thematic is: (1) rebellion and killing of the prophets; (2) punishment; (3) mercy through sending of new prophets; (4) sin and rejection of prophets. While the first part of the pattern is prominent in Luke 1–23, the second part dominates Luke 24 and Acts.[7] What is highlighted in this theme is not the prophet—his powers to speak for God, to heal a broken humanity, or to predict God's salvific will. The ''rejected prophet'' theme spotlights God, a compassionate and forgiving God whose endless mercy and fidelity to his creation is typified in his continued action of sending his messengers to a rebellious and sinful people.[8]

A splendid example of the motif of ''rejected prophet'' is found in the prayer of Nehemiah 9:26–31.[9] Elements of the pattern of the ''rejected prophet'' motif will be italicized. The reader should note carefully the Godward direction of this thematic:

> [26]Nevertheless they were disobedient and rebelled against you and cast your law behind their back and *killed your prophets*, who had warned them in order to turn them back to you, and they committed great blasphemies. [27]Therefore you gave them into the hand of their enemies, *who made them suffer*; and in the time of their suffering they cried to you and you heard them from heaven; and *according to your great mercies* you gave them saviors who saved them from the hand of their enemies.[28] But after they had rest *they did evil again* before you, and you abandoned them to the hand of their enemies, so that they had dominion over them; yet when they turned and cried to you you heard from heaven, and *many times you delivered them according to your mercies*. [29]And you warned them in

order to turn them back to your law. Yet they acted presump-
tuously and did not obey your commandments, but sinned
against your ordinances by the observance of which a man
shall live, and turned a stubborn shoulder and stiffened their
neck and would not obey. [30]Many years you bore with them,
and warned them by your Spirit *through your prophets*; yet
they would not give ear. Therefore you gave them into the
hand of the peoples of the lands. [31]Nevertheless in your great
mercies you did not make an end of them or forsake them; for
you are a gracious and merciful God.

As the reader reflects on this prayer passage again, I re-emphasize
two items about this retelling of God's dealings with his creation: (1) the
prophet's role is to call people back to the doing of God's will; (2) God
is faithful to his creation and will forgive. The theme of the "rejected
prophet" does not champion the unredeemable nature of the human person, but "the dauntless persistence of the divine will to forgive."[10]
A preliminary answer to the question with which we began this
chapter, then, is: Jesus, according to Luke's kerygmatic story, is God's
innocently suffering righteous one and God's rejected prophet, and by
being such got to the cross. In the following chapters we will fill in this
skeletal answer by showing the godly way of life Jesus the righteous person led and the nature of the divine message this prophet proclaimed.
The themes of justice and food aid Luke in his total portrayal of Jesus the
prophet and righteous one whose life and ministry are one of obedience
to the will of his faithful God.

NOTES

1. I do not give the themes of Jesus as prophet and Jesus as the righteous
one full and independent treatment in this book. I opine that these themes are an-
cillary to, although intimately related with, the more comprehensive themes of
the faithful God and justice. The following formulations of the interconnections
will adumbrate my reasons. I italicize the links. The rejection of *prophet* Jesus'
justice life-style puts his *faithful God* on trial. As *prophet* of this God, Jesus
preaches the good news of *God's fidelity* to his creation, to the poor who have no
place to turn for *justice*. As the embodiment of his God's kingly *justice*, Jesus,
the *righteous one*, dines with sinners and brings the wrath of the religious leaders
down on his head for this symbolic demonstration of *God's fidelity* to his crea-

tion. See Freedman, "The Literary Motif," 127–28 on motif as a "family or associational cluster." The reader is referred to Chapters Three and Five below for confirmation of the views merely presented here.

2. See G. Schrenk, *"Dike, ktl," TDNT* 2.189.

3. The usual translations (see NEB, NAB, RSV) of Luke 23:47 as in the RSV's "Certainly this man was innocent" are not fully accurate. See Brian E. Beck, " *'Imitatio Christi'* and the Lucan Passion Narrative," in *Suffering and Martyrdom in the New Testament: Studies presented to G.M. Styler by the Cambridge New Testament Seminar* (ed. William Horburg; Brian McNeil; Cambridge: Cambridge University, 1981) 40–46; Anton Buechele, *Der Tod Jesus im Lukasevangelium: Eine redaktionsgeschichtliche Untersuchung zu Lk 23* (Frankfurter Theologische Studien 26; Frankfurt am Main: Josef Knecht, 1978) 88–91. In our discussion of Luke 23, we will have occasion to see how Luke's programmatic Magnificat (1:46–55), especially 1:51–53, takes on new coloration when viewed from the perspective of Jesus as the suffering righteous one. Luke 1:51–53 uses terminology akin to that of the psalms of the suffering righteous one to talk about the divine reversal seen in the Savior to be born, e.g., in vindicating Jesus, the suffering righteous one, God will truly exalt those of low degree (1:52).

4. In reference to Wisdom 2–5, Eduard Schweizer (*Lordship and Discipleship* [SBT 1/28; London: SCM, 1960] 30) writes: "The way of the righteous one depicted here is even in many details the way which Jesus has actually gone."

5. The psalms of the suffering righteous person betimes end on a note of vengeance against the enemies of the righteous one. See, e.g., Psalm 69. The theme of the "rejected prophet," as we will see below, accentuates God's forgiveness of the enemies of his prophet. See Luke 23:34.

6. See the full listing of references to Jesus as prophet in Buechele, *Tod Jesu* 91–92. His first category of references is to passages where Jesus acts like a prophet although the text does not call him a prophet: Luke 9:22–23; 9:43b–45; 18:31–34; 11:20; 11:29–32; 11:50; 13:32,34; 19:41–44; 20:9–18; 21:20–24; 22:64; 23:28–30; 23:43; 24:19–20; Acts 3:22–23; 7:37–53. Buechele's second category concerns texts where Jesus uses the title "prophet" for himself: Luke 4:24; 13:33. His final category concerns texts which use the title of prophet to describe Jesus' power: Luke 7:16; 9:8–9; 9:19; 7:39. One should note how many of these texts underscore the rejection of the prophet Jesus.

7. For evidence that Luke was aware of this pattern and theme, see also Luke 6:22–23; 11:49–51; 13:34–35; Acts 7:35,51–52.

8. Note how Luke 23:34a is juxtaposed with 23:26–31: forgiveness after threat of punishment.

9. See also *Jub.* 1:12–18; 2 Kgs 17:13–14; 2 Chr 24:17–19; Josephus,

Antiquities 10.38 (see also 9.265–66). For further argumentation about the Lukan use of the theme of "rejected prophet," see Richard J. Dillon, "Easter Revelation and Mission Program in Luke 24:46–48," in *Sin, Salvation, and the Spirit: Commemorating the Fiftieth Year of The Liturgical Press* (ed. Daniel Durken; Collegeville: Liturgical Press, 1979) 240–70.

    10. Ibid., 250.

Chapter Three

THE THEME OF JUSTICE

In this chapter I want to flesh out the skeletal answer I provided last chapter to the question: How did Jesus get himself crucified? By means of the motif of justice[1] I will give greater nuance to my answer that Jesus got to the cross by being God's righteous one and God's prophet of good news to the poor.

Luke's theme of justice will be seen negatively and positively. Negatively, it will be seen in Jesus' non-violent confrontation with the teaching and life-style of the religious leaders. Positively, it will be seen in Jesus' life-style of preaching and doing God's kingly justice.

As both treatments proceed, my readers will note that the master theme of the faithful God will reappear time and again. They will also begin to realize that the religious leaders are types of persons who do not do justice, that is, people who do not care for the defenseless person, imaged biblically by the "widow," who do not perform the justice work of almsgiving,[2] are arrogant toward the lowly, and worship themselves rather than God.[3] These are the persons who, by Luke's narrative thematic twist, are sinners and unrighteous while all the time claiming to be righteous and just. Further, through Luke's presentation of the religious leaders the readers will begin to detect Luke's notion of sin as self-exaltation, greed, neglect of justice, and blindness to one's need for salvation.[4]

Before looking at representative passages of the theme of justice, I want to aid the reader with two additional points of guidance. The reader is encouraged to read and reread Luke-Acts, especially the Gospel. Within the compass of this book it is impossible to provide all the contexts for a particular theme. To the extent that the theme is seen within the flow of the entire Gospel of Luke, to that extent will the reader appreciate its rich contribution to the total tapestry of themes.[5] Secondly, in addition to footnote one above which contains much information about Luke's theme of justice, I would like to offer the reader the following, anticipatory, one-paragraph statement on Luke's motif of justice.

Jesus' ministry of calling sinners to righteous ways of life, e.g., almsgiving, is denounced by religious leaders who appear to be righteous. Jesus is the righteous one par excellence, who, obedient to God's will and plan, reveals and embodies that kingly plan. He reveals a God who is just to the poor and afflicted and thereby faithful to himself and his promises of life. Jesus unjustly meets with opposition from the religious leaders. As such, he is the innocently suffering righteous one, in whom God is on trial for his fidelity. God vindicates himself and his plan for creation in exalting the crucified righteous one, Jesus. When the centurion sees the mighty deed of God's fidelity to Jesus and Jesus' fidelity to his Father's plan, this pagan confesses that Jesus is indeed God's righteous one, his Son. Pagans and other outcasts, who should have no eyes, see whereas those who reputedly have superior insight into God's ways are blind.[6]

JESUS, GOD'S PROPHET AND RIGHTEOUS ONE, ATTACKS RELIGIOUS LEADERS FOR NOT DOING JUSTICE

In discussing Jesus' non-violent confrontation with the teaching and life-style of the religious leaders, I will limit myself to five representative texts:[7] Luke 7:29–30; 11:37–54; 16:14–18; 18:9–14; 20:45–21:6.

Luke 7:29–30

> [29]When they heard this all the people and the tax collectors justified God, having been baptized with the baptism of John; [30]but the Pharisees and the lawyers rejected the purpose of God for themselves, not having been baptized by him.

We begin with a passage from Jesus' Galilean ministry, which does not speak directly about Jesus,[8] but does speak tomes about God's justice and fidelity. Luke 7:29–30 occurs in a context of Jesus' evaluation of the ministry of John the Baptist. John's baptism was a symbolic act of

God's gift of salvation and of human need for such a gift. And in the Lukan context it is not surprising that John the Baptist demands deeds of justice from those who have symbolized by their submission to baptism that they are converted to a new view of God. Their actions will show that they are of Abraham, for they perform deeds conformable to the nature of the biblical God of justice. See Luke 3:10–14: ''And the multitudes asked him, 'What then shall we do?' And he answered them, 'He who has two coats, let him share with him who has none; and he who has food, let him do likewise.' Tax collectors also came to be baptized, and said to him, 'Teacher, what shall we do?' And he said to them, 'Collect no more than is appointed you.' Soldiers also asked him, 'And we, what shall we do?' And he said to them, 'Rob no one by violence or by false accusation, and be content with your wages.' ''

Tax collectors and other outcasts acknowledge their need of God and of repentance and therefore are baptized. But the religious leaders feel no such need. They do not accept God's righteousness; they do not accept the preachers of that righteousness—John and Jesus who are children of Wisdom (7:35). They have their own righteousness.[9]

The multitude (3:10) and the people (7:29) confess their trust in a faithful God and acknowledge God's plan for them and are won for God by John the Baptist. In Luke's Gospel ''the multitude'' (*ho ochlos*) and ''the people'' (*ho laos*) are quite interchangeable. The multitude/people in Luke's kerygmatic story are representative of those who are generally open to God's message, as proclaimed by Jesus the prophet, but are also subject to the baneful influence of the religious leaders.[10]

In summary, what is important is that Luke describes true conversion to God's plan of salvation as the doing of justice; non-conversion, as we shall see, means continued involvement in deeds of non-justice.

Luke 11:37–54

Sufficient for the purposes of this study is a brief examination of part of the larger passage—Luke 11:37–43:

> [37]While he was speaking, a Pharisee asked him to dine with him; so he went in and sat at table. [38]The Pharisee was astonished to see that he did not first wash before dinner. [39]And the Lord said to him, 'Now you Pharisees cleanse the outside of

> the cup and of the dish, but inside you are full of extortion and wickedness. [40]You fools! Did not he who made the outside make the inside also? [41]But give for alms those things which are within; and behold, everything is clean for you. [42]But woe to you Pharisees! for you tithe mint and rue and every herb, and neglect justice and the love of God; these you ought to have done, without neglecting the others. [43]Woe to you Pharisees! for you love the best seat in the synagogues and salutations in the market places.'

In a context of sharing food (11:37) and therefore sharing life[11] and in a context of teaching God's way of life as he obediently journeys to Jerusalem (9:51–19:44), Jesus here attacks the life-style of the Pharisees.

Justice in the form of almsgiving is more important than ritual cleansing before sharing the food of life (11:41). "Extortion" (11:39)[12] will be cleansed, not by washing before a meal, but by caring for the needy from the heart.[13]

The representative Pharisees are given another prophetic challenge to repent because they have neglected justice and the love of God (11:42). They are full of pride as they seek human adulation (11:43).[14]

Be it noted that in 11:37–43 the implicit norm of judgment against the Pharisees is that they have not done works of justice: no almsgiving;[15] no acknowledgment of God's rights over them and consequently of their dependence on him. On the contrary, these religious leaders seize goods from others by extortion and search after pedestals of human glory. After this confrontation with Jesus, they lie "in wait for him, to catch at something he might say" (11:54).

Luke 16:14–18

Luke 16:14–18 presents a potential volume of exegetical concerns. For our purposes it is sufficient to concentrate on 16:14–15 and to note that this passage occurs as Jesus makes his way to Jerusalem and is teaching about possessions (see 16:1–13 and 16:19–31):

> [14]The Pharisees, who were lovers of money, heard all this, and they scoffed at him. [15]But he said to them, 'You are those who justify yourselves before men, but God knows your hearts; for

what is exalted among men is an abomination in the sight of God.'

The Pharisees hear all of Jesus' teaching about the necessity of almsgiving (16:9).[16] They are characterized as "lovers of money" and as "scoffing" at Jesus' teaching about the proper use of possessions.[17] Besides this characterization of "greedy" which links up well with "extortion" in 11:39, the Pharisees are said to "justify" themselves (see 18:9–14). Their righteousness is their own; they have no need of God (see also 14:11; 18:14). They are truly righteous. In considering Luke 23:47 in the context of Luke's entire Gospel, Brian Beck makes a provocative observation about the "certainly" (*ontōs*) of "Certainly this man was righteous" (23:47). He writes: "There may even be a particular point in the adverb *ontōs* ("certainly"). In more than one place Luke refers caustically to those whose righteousness is feigned or based only on self-esteem (16:15; 18:9; 20:20); in Jesus we see the genuine thing."[18]

Luke 18:9–14

> [9]He also told this parable to some who trusted in themselves that they were righteous and despised others: [10]"Two men went up into the temple to pray, one a Pharisee and the other a tax collector. [11]The Pharisee stood and prayed thus with himself, "God, I thank thee that I am not like other men, extortioners, unjust, adulterers, or even like this tax collector. [12]I fast twice a week, I give tithes of all that I get." [13]But the tax collector, standing far off, would not even lift up his eyes to heaven, but beat his breast, saying, "God, be merciful to me a sinner!" [14]I tell you, this man went down to his house justified rather than the other; for every one who exalts himself will be humbled, but he who humbles himself will be exalted.'

Our consideration of Luke 7:29–30 has primed us to see 18:9–14 in its proper light. In this example story the Pharisee is pitted over against a member of Luke's rogues' gallery. As in 7:29–30, the question is one of justice. The tax collector, against all religious expectations, is open to God and confesses his needy status. The Pharisee is the negative example of persons who justify themselves rather than rely on God's justice. It is with supreme irony that Luke has the Pharisee pray that he is not an extortioner (18:11). In Luke 11:39 we have the only other Lukan occurrence of the same basic word, "extortion." The Pharisees are not examples of the righteous person who has been humbled and yet maintains trust in a gracious and faithful God. They exalt themselves at the cost of the dignity and human rights of others.

In 18:9–14 we again see that the religious leaders are painted with the colors of the deeds of non-justice. They have no room for the justice of God which is manifesting itself in Jesus' kingdom ministry.

Luke 20:45–21:6

In the two previous major sections of Luke's Gospel (4:14–9:50; 9:51–19:44) Luke has presented Jesus in non-violent confrontation with the religious leaders. It is to be expected then that Jesus will be described as confronting the religious leaders in Luke's final section (19:45–24:53), a section which deals with the rejection of the prophet Jesus by Jerusalem which kills prophets (see 13:33–35). Luke 20:45–21:6 occurs at the end of a series of controversies which began with Jesus' prophetic cleansing of the temple as a sign of God's destruction of it because the religious leaders had not performed deeds of justice (see 19:45–49):

> 45And in the hearing of all the people he said to his disciples, 46'Beware of the scribes, who like to go about in long robes, and love salutations in the market places and the best seats in their synagogues and the places of honor at feasts, 47who devour widows' houses and for a pretense make long prayers. They will receive the greater condemnation.' 1He looked up and saw the rich putting their gifts into the treasury; 2and he saw a poor widow put in two copper coins. 3And he said, 'Truly I tell you, this poor widow has put in more than all of them; 4for they all contributed out of their abundance, but she out of her poverty put in all the living that she had.' 5And as some spoke of the temple, how it was adorned with noble stones and offerings, he said, 6'As for these things which you see, the days will come when there shall not be left here one stone upon another that will not be thrown down.'

Jesus the prophet pronounces judgment against the religious leaders for their pride and lack of justice to the weakest members of society, the widows (20:47).[19] In contrast to the prodigal son who squandered his "living" and abandoned God (15:12–13:30), the widow of 21:1–4 gives all her "living" (21:4) to God. She is a model of generosity and is contrasted with the rich (21:1–3). Her generosity prepares the reader to appreciate that of Jesus who self-effacingly serves others (22:24–27) as he steadfastly journeys to his faithful Father via the cross. Her generosity stands in marked contrast to the greed of Judas who will abandon Jesus' journey of justice and go over to the side of the religious leaders for the sake of money (22:1–5).[20] She stands also in stark contrast to a way of life which ignores God's justice and finds security in beautifully adorned buildings dedicated to God (21:5–6).[21]

This entire section on Jesus' attacks against religious leaders can be summed up in this way. The religious leaders will reject Jesus. In the language of Luke 9:22: "The Son of man must suffer many things, and be rejected by the elders and chief priests and scribes, and be killed, and on the third day be raised." They reject him because of his strictures on their way of life. But these religious leaders are not those of the days of Jesus of Nazareth.[22] Nor are they the Christian Pharisees of Luke's communities.[23] They are stereotypes of persons who do not respond to the ways of the faithful God in Jesus.[24] These folks are also living symbols of the Lukan view of sin. They do not do justice, that is, do not care for defenseless people, are arrogant toward societal and religious outcasts, and worship at the shrine of self rather than at the shrine of the God of justice. Their hostility mounts until they cannot wait to put Jesus to death (22:2). Before Pilate they will cry out for Jesus' crucifixion (23:13–25). And Jesus will pray for their forgiveness (23:34).

In the next section we will have occasion to see how Luke paints the justice life-style of Jesus, the righteous one and prophet of God's good news to the poor.

JESUS' LIFE-STYLE OF JUSTICE

It is impossible to explore this vast topic in detail. Highlights will have to suffice. After arguing that the symbol, "kingdom of God," involves the "doing of justice," I will move to a consideration of the following representative texts: Luke 4:16–30; 13:11–17; 18:18–30; 22:47–53.

The scholarly world is in debt to the late Norman Perrin for his insistence that the kingdom of God is a symbol.[25] It is a symbol that God is king and ruler over chaos, over the powers of evil and injustice at work in his world. God, the righteous ruler, will conquer evil.

And as a symbol, the kingdom of God is polyvalent. And one of its valences is God's justice.[26] The correlation between God's justice and his kingly rule is very clear in Psalm 97:1–2: "The Lord reigns; let the earth rejoice; let the many coastlands be glad! Clouds and thick darkness are round about him; righteousness and justice are the foundation of his throne."[27]

Jesus, as the preacher and effector of God's kingdom, reveals God's work of justice. Johannes Nuetzel has made a sound point by showing how Luke 4:43, a key passage for Luke's description of Jesus' mission, is related to its context.[28] Luke 4:43 reads: "But he said to them, 'I must preach the good news of the kingdom of God to the other cities also; for I was sent for this purpose.' " The literary context of 4:43 contains 4:16–30 which speaks of Jesus the prophet being anointed by God to fulfill his promises by preaching good news to the poor (4:18). The summary statement of Jesus' mission in 4:43 as preaching the good news of the kingdom involves his justice work of preaching good news to the poor.

Once the reader begins to see the intimate connection between the kingdom of God and God's justice, other kingdom passages take on new meaning. See, for example, 6:20: "And he lifted up his eyes on his disciples and said: 'Blessed are you poor, for yours is the kingdom of God.' " God is the faithful king as he rights the human situation where injustice and oppression reign. See also Luke 11:20: "But if it is by the finger of God that I cast out demons, then the kingdom of God has come upon you." Demons, symbols of the power of evil in human life, mock the fidelity and justice of a God who creates goodness. By casting demons out, Jesus shows the justice of a faithful God who will not let evil have the final say over his creation. As we will see in detail subsequently, Luke 23 has much to say about Jesus as King. Jesus' kind of kingship, predicted to Mary and the reader in 1:32–33, is interpreted by his life and death for justice. In 23:42 Jesus continues God's kingly justice by promising life to the criminal who repentantly asks him to remember him when he comes in his kingly power. Finally, Luke ends his two volumes in Acts 28 with two passages which identify God's kingdom with Jesus. See 28:31: Paul is "preaching the kingdom of God and teaching about the Lord Jesus Christ quite openly and unhindered" (see also 28:23). God's justice is to be found in Jesus' life, death, and resurrection. All his promises to rectify the human condition have come true in Jesus.[29] He is the faithful God.

Luke 4:16–30

[16]And he came to Nazareth, where he had been brought up; and he went to the synagogue, as his custom was, on the sabbath day. And he stood up to read; [17]and there was given to him the book of the prophet Isaiah. He opened the book and found the place where it was written, [18]'The Spirit of the Lord is upon me, because he has anointed me to preach good news to the poor. He has sent me to proclaim release to the captives and recovering of sight to the blind, to set at liberty those who are oppressed, [19]to proclaim the acceptable year of the Lord.' [20]And he closed the book, and gave it back to the attendant, and sat down; and the eyes of all in the synagogue were fixed on him. [21]And he began to say to them, 'Today this scripture has been fulfilled in your hearing.' [22]And all spoke well of him, and wondered at the gracious words which proceeded out of his mouth; and they said 'Is not this Joseph's son?' [23]And he said to them, 'Doubtless you will quote to me this proverb, "Physician, heal yourself, what we have heard you did at Capernaum, do here also in your own country."' [24]And he said, 'Truly, I say to you, no prophet is acceptable in his own country. [25]But in truth, I tell you, there were many widows in Israel in the days of Elijah, when the heaven was shut up three years and six months, when there came a great famine over all the land; [26]and Elijah was sent to none of them but only to Zarephath, in the land of Sidon, to a woman who was a widow. [27]And there were many lepers in Israel in the time of the prophet Elisha; and none of them was cleansed, but only Naaman the Syrian.' [28]When they heard this, all in the synagogue were filled with wrath. [29]And they rose up and put him out of

the city, and led him to the brow of the hill on which their city was built, that they might throw him down headlong. [30]But passing through the midst of them he went away.

In this programmatic text we will limit ourselves to three basic considerations. First, what is the meaning of "the poor" in 4:18 (and throughout the rest of Luke's Gospel)? In my literary approach to Luke's Gospel I build upon the insights of Michael Guinan,[30] Luke Johnson,[31] and Walter Pilgrim[32] and define "the poor" as those who cannot demand justice for themselves and trust in the justice of God, especially as revealed in the Christ event.[33] Thus, the barren Elizabeth (1:5–25) is poor; the widow of Nain is poor (7:11–17); and all others whose situations seem beyond rectifying are poor. Luke 4:16–30 announces the heart of Jesus' entire ministry. In him the God of justice is active for the poor. What had been the expectation of all people is now being fulfilled in Jesus. Luke projects in 4:16–30 a God who is faithful to his promises, faithful to his creation, a God who is for justice. In Jesus, Luke's kerygmatic story proclaims, God is for all people and against all forms of evil, all forms of poverty and hunger. Can the reader believe in this God?

The second point for comment in Luke 4:16–30 also occurs in 4:18. In 4:18 two English words translate the same Greek word: "release" and "at liberty" translate the Greek *aphesis*. This Greek word is derived from ancient economy and social relations and is an image of release from debts or imprisonment.[34] It images God as the judge to whom human beings are responsible.[35] When the imagery behind this use of *aphesis* becomes focused in this way, one begins to see that the passage talks about a God whose justice is prodigal. In his justice this God generously releases his creation from the debt of guilt. In his ministry Jesus embodies God's work of justice by granting release/forgiveness from sins.[36]

"To proclaim release to the captives and to set at liberty those who are oppressed" points ahead to Luke 23. On the cross Jesus prays for his enemies that his Father release them from their sins (23:34). By his death on the cross Jesus liberates Barabbas, a murderer and insurrectionist, from prison (23:18,25). Jesus' death grants release from prison not just to the noble and beautiful, but also and especially to the scum of society. Still another way that 4:18 is programmatic is detected in 24:47: "and that repentance and forgiveness (*aphesis*) of sins should be preached in his name to all nations, beginning from Jerusalem.'' Jesus is proclaimed as the one in whom God's generous justice frees human beings from the debt of sin which keeps them away from concourse with God.[37] In Jesus God is faithful to his creation and communes with his creatures.

In brief, in Jesus' ministry, God shows that his justice far exceeds a tit-for-tat relationship. He generously forgives when there is no reason for such forgiveness.[38]

The final observation on 4:16–30 deals with its message of universality. The townspeople do not tolerate a God who in the ministry of Jesus the prophet will go out to social and religious outcasts as he did to a pagan widow and leper through his prophets, Elijah and Elisha (4:25–27). They reject this type of message and want to destroy its messenger. But they are unable. No one can destroy this prophet of justice, whom God will vindicate as his genuine messenger by raising him from the dead.[39]

Luke 13:10–17

This passage occurs in Luke's travel narrative (9:51–19:44) which describes Jesus as obediently living out his journey to the Father, which will become his disciples' way of life. His way of justice meets head-on with opposition from a religious leader while the people are open to see God's justice at work in Jesus' ministry (13:17).

> [10]Now he was teaching in one of the synagogues on the sabbath. [11]And there was a woman who had had a spirit of infirmity for eighteen years; she was bent over and could not fully straighten herself. [12]And when Jesus saw her, he called her and said to her, 'Woman, you are freed from your infirmity.' [13]And he laid his hands upon her, and immediately she was made straight, and she praised God. [14]But the ruler of the synagogue, indignant because Jesus had healed on the sabbath, said to the people, 'There are six days on which work ought to be done; come on those days and be healed, and not on the sabbath day.' [15]Then the Lord answered him, 'You hypocrites! Does not each of you on the sabbath untie his ox or his ass from the manger, and lead it away to water it? [16]And ought

> not this woman, a daughter of Abraham whom Satan bound
> for eighteen years, be loosed from this bond on the sabbath
> day?' [17]As he said this, all his adversaries were put to shame;
> and all the people rejoiced at all the glorious things that were
> done by him.

Jesus does merciful justice for a person who cannot demand justice for
herself. Verse eleven graphically describes her impossible situation.
And as verse sixteen adds, Satan has held her bound for these eighteen
years. Jesus, who has come to grant release from bondage (4:18), liberates this poor person. He gives her life on the sabbath, a day which
was meant to celebrate the giving of life.

This indigent woman is a daughter of Abraham (13:16). A brief
glance at the thematic of "children of Abraham" in Luke's Gospel will
reveal the full impact of this statement. From 1:54–55 to 3:7–9 and
through 16:22–31 and onto 19:9, the question rings out: Who is a child
of Abraham and thus heir to God's promises made to Abraham? This
woman, like the wretched poor man of 16:19–31 and like the despised
tax collector Zacchaeus in 19:1–10, is a child of Abraham. She is such
because of God's fidelity to himself and to his promises (1:54–55),[40] and
almost more importantly because of God's mercy to those who are
judged not to belong to God's chosen ones.

This last point touches upon another Lukan theme: how Jesus reveals God's justice by breaking through the narrow confines of human
justice and caring for an outcast class in society—women.[41] The universalism of God's justice in Jesus, which includes men and women in its
merciful sweep, recurs in Luke 23:49, which narrates that faithful
women disciples witness Jesus' death. And Luke 24:1–12 will tell of
their role as proclaimers of God's raising up of the prophet Jesus.[42]

Luke 18:18–30

> [18]And a ruler asked him, 'Good Teacher, what shall I do to in-
> herit eternal life?' [19]And Jesus said to him, 'Why do you call
> me good? No one is good but God alone. [20]You know the com-
> mandments: "Do not commit adultery, Do not kill, Do not
> steal, Do not bear false witness, Honor your father and
> mother."' [21]And he said, 'All these I have observed from my

youth.' [22]And when Jesus heard it, he said to him, 'One thing you still lack. Sell all that you have and distribute to the poor, and you will have treasure in heaven; and come, follow me.' [23]But when he heard this he became sad, for he was very rich. [24]Jesus looking at him said, 'How hard it is for those who have riches to enter the kingdom of God! [25]For it is easier for a camel to go through the eye of a needle than for a rich man to enter the kingdom of God.' [26]Those who heard it said, 'Then who can be saved?' [27]But he said, 'What is impossible with men is possible with God.' [28]And Peter said, 'Lo, we have left our homes and followed you.' [29]And he said to them, 'Truly, I say to you, there is no man who has left house or wife or brothers or parents or children, for the sake of the kingdom of God, [30]who will not receive manifold more in this time, and in the age to come eternal life.'

As Jesus is completing his revelation[43] of God's will as a way of life which leads to salvation, he is met by one of the religious leaders.[44] The religious leader is challenged to adopt a life-style of justice (18:22)[45] and to follow Jesus who helps the helpless, those who cannot demand justice for themselves. By following Jesus, the religious leader will inherit eternal life and gain entry into God's reign of justice.

People are amazed (18:26–27) that a rich person is not a sure candidate for membership in God's society of justice and ask: "Then who can be saved?" Jesus answers the startled questioners by giving further nuance to his teaching on a life-style of care for the helpless. His answer echoes the angel's response to Mary: "For with God nothing will be impossible" (1:37). God will fulfill his promises of giving new life even when people and conditions seem incapable of life. God is faithful although human beings may doubt that there is any basis for fulfillment or may abandon the way of justice or may find in possessions a sign of human accomplishment and of acceptability before God. God will share freely his just graciousness, but in his own way as the disciples will learn as Luke's kerygmatic story develops.[46]

Peter, a spokesperson for all disciples, is a living example that abandoning all (5:11) and following Jesus' life-style are possible. But as Peter's temporary forsaking of Jesus' way will show (22:54–62), following Jesus and trying to comprehend God's ways in Jesus, the righteous one and prophet of God's good news to the poor, are fraught with difficulties. At the crucifixion a repentant Peter and the other male disciples will be present.[47] They will see the death of God's righteous one, Jesus. And as Luke will narrate in chapter 24, the disciples, with eyes opened to faith by the risen Jesus,[48] will see that what seemed impossible to humankind is possible with God: the faithful and just God has vindicated Jesus, the poor person par excellence, who lived and died for God's justice.[49]

Luke 22:47–53

> [47]While he was still speaking, there came a crowd, and the man called Judas, one of the twelve, was leading them. He drew near to Jesus to kiss him; [48]but Jesus said to him, 'Judas, would you betray the Son of man with a kiss?' [49]And when those who were about him saw what would follow, they said, 'Lord, shall we strike with the sword?' [50]And one of them struck the slave of the high priest and cut off his right ear. [51]But Jesus said, 'No more of this!' And he touched his ear and healed him. [52]Then Jesus said to the chief priests and captains of the temple and elders, who had come out against him, 'Have you come out as against a robber, with swords and clubs? [53]When I was with you day after day in the temple, you did not lay hands on me. But this is your hour, and the power of darkness.'

This passage describes Jesus on the brink of his passion and calls for brief comments.

Judas, the one who represents those who abandon Jesus' way of justice for money (22:1–5), tries to betray Jesus with a sign of friendship. He is on the side of the religious leaders, on the side of darkness.

Jesus' healing of the ear of the slave of the high priest not only is the culmination of Jesus' life of healing mercy, but also and especially embodies his life-style of love of enemies,[50] and anticipates his prayer of forgiveness from the cross for his enemies (23:34). Jesus' confrontation with his adversaries, the religious leaders, had as its goal to lead to justice and peace in society.[51] Following Jesus is laden with potential conflict as the imagery of the swords of 22:35–38 already indicated. But disciples misunderstand Jesus' way of justice if they adopt a course of violence (22:51).[52]

With 22:47–53 the fulfillment of Jesus' prediction in 9:22 is coming to pass: "The Son of man must suffer many things, and be rejected by the elders and chief priests and scribes, and be killed, and on the third day be raised." Jesus, the righteous one, has strengthened his fidelity to his Father through prayer (see 22:39–46). He freely moves forward in obedience to his Father's will[53] to confront "the power of darkness" (22:53) represented in the religious leaders, who have come to kill the righteous person. And in attacking God's righteous one, they are also attacking the faithful God who wills to vindicate those who labor for justice and those who suffer unjustly. In Luke's description of Jesus' death on the cross the power of evil will be explicitly reintroduced by the symbol of darkness (23:44–45). In Jesus' crucifixion the power of injustice will confront the power of justice. The light of the early dawn of God's new week of creation will show which power was victorious (24:1).

CONCLUSION TO CHAPTER THREE

This entire chapter on Luke's theme of justice has shown how Jesus was God's prophet of justice and by being such got himself crucified. By his life of preaching and being good news to those who could claim no justice for themselves, he truly was a righteous person. And as such, his life contrasted diametrically with that of religious leaders, who professed to be righteous. Jesus attacked them verbally for not effecting justice. And his very way of life was an affront to them.

Pursuit of Luke's theme of justice has, indeed, given us readers more information on why Jesus got himself crucified. He died because of his vision of God. He was crucified because he proclaimed in word and deed a God whose nature as a faithful, just, forgiving, and merciful God demanded the same type of conduct from his worshipers. In Jesus the kingly justice of this God was being revealed to a needy and battered creation. The response to this revelation was mixed. Religious leaders, symbols of persons whose lives are generally closed in on themselves and believe that they have a corner on God's love, rejected Jesus' vision of the faithful God and of his role in realizing that vision. Tax collectors, symbols of social and religious outcasts, are open to Jesus' vision of God, eagerly do justice, and sit down with Jesus at table and make merry. The "multitudes" and "the people" are generally open to hear Jesus' vision of God, to praise the God at work in Jesus' ministry, and to repent by doing works of justice. Can readers of Luke's kerygmatic story believe in this God, whose righteous one and prophet was earmarked for the cross because he bodied forth such a God?

Luke 23 will answer the question with which we end this chapter: Will the God, in whom Jesus believed so strongly and whose way of justice he effected so rigorously, be faithful to him at his last hours and deliver him from his adversaries? Or put in the words of the oppressors of God's righteous one: "Let us lie in wait for the righteous man, because he is inconvenient to us and opposes our actions. . . . If the righteous man is God's son, he will help him, and will deliver him from the hand of his adversaries" (Wis 2:12,18).

NOTES

1. Some summary statistics and evaluation of Luke's theme of justice will show how predominant this theme is in Luke. The statistics are as follows. Of the Gospels only Matthew has more instances of the basic Greek word for "justice" (*dikai-*). "Justice/righteousness" (*dikaiosynē*) occurs once in Luke's Gospel and six times in Acts. "Righteous/just" (*dikaios*) occurs eleven times in the Gospel and six times in Acts. "To make righteous/to justify" (*dikaioō*) occurs five times in the Gospel and twice in Acts. In the Gospel "commandment" (*dikaiōma*) occurs once as does "justly" (*dikaiōs*). See John Reumann, *"Righteousness" in the New Testament: "Justification" in the United States Lutheran-Roman Catholic Dialogue. With responses by Joseph A. Fitzmyer and Jerome D. Quinn* (Philadelphia: Fortress; New York/Ramsey: Paulist, 1982) 135 (#244).

On pp. 142–43 (#253) Reumann presents a summary of the thematic of justice in Luke-Acts. It should be noted that Reumann has investigated Luke-Acts from the perspective of whether its teaching on righteousness shows Pauline influence. Since his treatment is one of the few on Luke's theme of righteousness, I will quote his entire summary: "But Luke-Acts does demonstrate how pervasive the terms were from OT roots. False claims at being *dikaios* were opposed (Luke 10:29; 16:15; 18:9; cf. 5:32). God's righteousness is vindicated (Luke 7:29), through Jesus and the response of sinners and publicans to him (Luke 7:35). He is 'the Righteous One' (Acts 3:14; 7:52; 22:14). That he taught how the humble and self-effacing, in contrast to the boastful, get to be 'justified' is recorded (Luke 18:14). Through Jesus one is justified in the sense of freed or exonerated, in ways the law of Moses could not provide (Acts 13:38–39). There is also ample reference to future resurrection of the 'just (and unjust)' (Luke 14:14; Acts 24:25), future judgment (Acts 17:31), and ethics in light thereof (Acts 24:25). This is not Paul's view, but a different sort developed in Gentile Christianity, from the gospel and OT traditions, but in the light of the Christ-event.'' In the representative passages treated below we will explore many of the passages Reumann discussed. Our angle of vision will be that of Luke, however, and not that of Paul.

2. On "justice as almsgiving," see John R. Donahue, "Biblical Perspectives on Justice," *The Faith That Does Justice: Examining the Christian Sources for Social Change* (ed. J.C. Haughey; Woodstock Studies 2; New York: Paulist, 1977) 84–85. Donahue documents how the Hebrew word for "justice" (*sedaqah*) came to be translated by "almsgiving" (*eleēmosynē*) in Greek. He writes: "This development represents a very important facet of biblical thought which was obscured by later distinctions between justice and charity. Concern for the poor and a desire to lessen the inequality between rich and poor either individually or collectively, in a biblical perspective, should not proceed simply from a love for or compassion with the sufferings of others, but is rooted in claims of justice, i.e., how one can be faithful to the Lord who has given the goods of the earth as common possession of all and be faithful to others in the human community who have equal claim to these goods'' (pp. 84–85). For a helpful treatment of the biblical notion of "almsgiving," see Luke T. Johnson, *Sharing Possessions: Mandate and Symbol of Faith* (Overtures to Biblical Theology; Philadelphia: Fortress, 1981) 132–39.

3. See Johnson, *Sharing Possessions* 79–116 and Michael D. Guinan, *Gospel Poverty: Witness to the Risen Christ, A Study in Biblical Spirituality* (New York: Paulist, 1981) 38–44. Both Johnson and Guinan are excellent in exposing the prophetic insight that injustice leads one away from the God of the covenant and that injustice itself is an act of idolatry, a denial of the God who has a passionate love for the needy and calls upon his covenant people to embody a similar love. Guinan writes: "Mistreatment of others flows from worshiping false gods. The prophets speak out against idolatry, forsaking the Lord, and against the form in which this manifests itself toward others: social injustice" (p. 43).

4. In what follows I am indebted to the insights of Jacques Dupont, *Les béatitudes, Tome III: Les évangélistes* (EBib; Paris: Gabalda, 1973) 19–206, esp. 149–203; Luke T. Johnson, *The Literary Function of Possessions in Luke-Acts.*

5. Readers who want to obtain an overall view of the structure and theology of Luke-Acts are referred to: Robert J. Karris, *What Are They Saying About Luke and Acts?* and Luke T. Johnson, *Luke-Acts: A Story of Prophet and People* (Herald Biblical Booklets; Chicago: Franciscan Herald, 1981).

6. In formulating this paragraph, I am indebted to Gloeckner, *Verkuendigung des Heils*, 187–91, 194–95. There is an excellent summary of pp. 155–95 of Gloeckner's monograph in Jerome Kodell, "Luke's Theology of the Death of Jesus," in *Sin, Salvation, and the Spirit*, 221–30.

7. In using the nomenclature of "representative texts," I indicate that the motif of justice occurs in all the significant contexts within Luke's Gospel. See Freedman, "The Literary Motif," 126–27.

8. Luke 7:29–30 anticipates 20:1–8 wherein the reaction of the religious leaders to Jesus the prophet resembles their reaction to the prophetic action of John the Baptist.

9. On the meaning of "justified God" (7:29) see Fitzmyer, *Luke* 676: "Lit. 'justified God,' i.e. acknowledged God as righteous, or acknowledged God's way of righteousness. The sense is that, in listening to John's preaching and in accepting his baptism for the remission of sins, people were acknowledging what God had done to establish righteousness in the world of human beings and to enable them to attain it in his sight. Their actions, in effect, rendered a verdict of approval on God's plan of salvation." As we will have occasion to see many times during the course of this study, the theme of justice is vital to Luke and runs throughout his entire Gospel, beginning in 1:6 with his description of the future parents of John the Baptist, hitting its high point in the centurion's confession of Jesus as a righteous person (23:47) and in God's justification/vindication of the suffering righteous one, who is his Son, in the resurrection. See Reumann, *"Righteousness,"* 135–43 (#244–53) on how pervasive the theme of justice is in Luke-Acts.

10. I realize that my way of reading the Lukan fluid terminology of "multitude" and "the people" goes against some current scholarly opinion. Let it be recalled that I am not trying to argue from the Lukan Gospel to Luke's life situation. Let it also be recalled that authors who champion the view that by "the people" (*ho laos*) Luke means God's chosen people must deal with troublesome "exception" passages like Luke 23:13. See Jerome Kodell, "Luke's Use of Laos, 'People,' especially in the Jerusalem Narrative (Lk 19,28–24,53)," *CBQ* 31 (1969) 327–43; Paul S. Minear, "Jesus' Audiences According to Luke," *NovT* 16 (1974) 81–109, esp. p. 86; see also Conzelmann, *Theology of St Luke* 164 n. 1 who argues for the identity of "multitude" and "people." What is important in all this discussion is that the religious leaders are separated from the multitude/people. The latter, despite their rejection of Jesus (23:13), are still open to hear God's message and to repent; see especially 23:35,48. But one should not think that the religious leaders are so identified with evil that they cannot be open to God's word of life. Note the peculiarly Lukan description of Joseph of Arimathea: "He was a member of the council, a good and righteous man, who had not consented to their purpose and deed, and he was looking for

the kingdom of God'' (23:50–51). This description stands in logical tension with 22:70 and 23:1 which stress that *all* members of the council acted against Jesus. This tension is resolved when the reader recalls that on a literary-theological level Luke may be trying to break our rigid categories of who is saint and sinner by saying that human perversity is never so complete that there are no righteous people, people who await the manifestation of God's kingly rule of justice, which in Luke takes place preeminently in Jesus' life, death, and exaltation. See Chapter One above, esp. the section on "Reflections on Motif."

11. See Chapter Four below on suggestions as to how the themes of justice and food are interrelated.

12. See Luke 18:11 where the Pharisee prides himself for not being an "extortioner."

13. On Luke 11:41, see I. Howard Marshall, *The Gospel of Luke: A Commentary on the Greek Text* (New International Greek Testament Commentary; Grand Rapids: Eerdmans, 1978) 495: "If men give alms, then everything will be clean. If the Pharisees overcome their rapacity, i.e. their inward uncleanness, then they will be fully clean, and ritual washing will presumably not be necessary."

14. See also Luke 14:11 and the similar description given of the "scribes" in 20:46.

15. See n. 2 above.

16. On Luke 16:9, see Marshall, *Luke* 621: "Hence the meaning is 'world wealth', as opposed to heavenly treasure. It is to be used to win friends, no doubt by almsgiving."

17. Might it be pure coincidence that the only other time Luke uses the word "scoff" is at the crucifixion, 23:35, where the religious leaders "scoff" at Jesus and ask him to save himself? Note also the "avoidability" factor in this occurrence of the motif. The word "greedy" occurs only one other time in the NT, in 2 Tim 3:2. The Greek is *philargyroi*.

18. " '*Imitatio Christi*,' " 46.

19. See the other places in Luke's Gospel in which this symbol of the weakest members of society is used: 2:37; 4:25,26: 7:12; 18:3,5.

20. For a superb treatment of the function of Judas in Luke-Acts, see Schuyler Brown, *Apostasy and Perseverance in the Theology of Luke* (AnBib 36; Rome: Pontifical Biblical Institute, 1969) 82–97.

21. Might Jeremiah 7:1–11, which lies behinds 19:46's "den of robbers" quotation, also be alluded to in 21:5–6? Recall that in Jer 7:1–11, people find security in God's temple and do not do the deeds of God, namely, do not care for widows (Jer 7:6). See Addison G. Wright, "The Widow's Mites: Praise or Lament?—A Matter of Context," *CBQ* 44 (1982) 256–65. Wright argues that Jesus is lamenting what the scribes have taught widows to do, namely, give their

sustenance to support a temple which, because of corruption, is going to be torn down stone by stone. Although he argues strongly for a "lament" interpretation, Wright does allow for my "praise" interpretation which sees the widow's gift in terms of the "cost for the giver" (p. 257). Besides raising an important point for the interpretation of this individual passage, Wright has implicitly called upon both Markan and Lukan scholars to explore in more detail the controversies of Jesus' last days in Jerusalem. An excellent start has been made on the Markan materials by Joanna Dewey, *Markan Public Debate: Literary Technique, Concentric Structure, and Theology in Mark 2:1–3:6* (SBLDS 48; Chico: Scholars, 1980) 152–66. It is my contention, which I do not have the space to argue here, that both Mark and Luke use the "destruction of Jerusalem" motif and the non-justice conduct of the religious leaders as means of teaching their readers lessons about discipleship. This is more clear in Mark than in Luke, but see Luke 20:45: "and in the hearing of all the people he said to his *disciples.*"

22. On the question of the "historical" Pharisees at the time of Jesus of Nazareth, see the evaluation that this question is "practically insoluble" in Michael J. Cook, "Jesus and the Pharisees—The Problem As It Stands Today," *JES* 15 (1978) 441–60.

23. With regard to the Pharisees and Luke's life situation, I do not find convincing the thesis of J.A. Ziesler that Luke favors the Pharisees. See his "Luke and the Pharisees," *NTS* 25 (1978/79) 146–57. See Johnson, *Literary Function*, 116 n. 3: "The case for Luke's favorable treatment of the Pharisees remains to be proven; it definitely should not be assumed"; see further pp. 109–10, 141–43, and passim.

24. On the narrative function of the Pharisees in the Gospels and Acts, see Jacob Neusner, *From Politics to Piety: The Emergence of Pharisaic Judaism* (Englewood Cliffs: Prentice-Hall, 1973) 72: the Pharisees of the New Testament "serve as a narrative convention. Whenever the narrator needs someone to ask a question that allows a stunning response on the part of Jesus, he calls forth the Pharisees. When a villain is needed to exemplify obviously unsavory spiritual traits he calls forth the Pharisees."

25. See his *Jesus and the Language of the Kingdom: Symbol and Metaphor in New Testament Interpretation* (Philadelphia: Fortress, 1976) 15–32.

26. In Freedman's terminology, the motif is a family or associational cluster. See his "The Literary Motif," 127–28.

27. For more detail on the link between the kingdom of God and God's justice, see Guinan, *Gospel Poverty* 26–31; Donahue, "Biblical Perspectives on Justice," 86–87; Reumann, *"Righteousness"*, 12–26 (#27–54), esp. 23–24 (#50–51).

28. See *Jesus als Offenbarer Gottes nach den Inkanischen* (sic) *Schriften* (Forschung zur Bibel 39; Wuerzburg: Echter, 1980) 28–30.

29. For more information about the identification of the kingdom of God with Jesus, see Otto Merk, "Das Reich Gottes in den lukanischen Schriften," in *Jesus und Paulus: Festschrift fuer Werner Georg Kuemmel zum 70. Geburtstag* (ed. E. Earle Ellis; Erich Graesser; Goettingen: Vandenhoeck & Ruprecht, 1975) 201–20; Dillon, *Eye-Witnesses* 286–87 n. 155; J. Dupont, "La conclusion des Actes et son rapport à l'ensemble de l'ouvrage de Luc," in *Les Actes des Apôtres: Traditions, rédaction, théologie* (ed. J. Kremer; BETL 48; Gembloux: Duculot/Leuven: University Press, 1979) 364–65.

30. *Gospel Poverty.*

31. *Sharing Possessions.*

32. *Good News to the Poor: Wealth and Poverty in Luke-Acts* (Minneapolis: Augsburg, 1981).

33. There are, of course, other approaches to who "the poor" are in Luke's Gospel. I will map them out in the excursus which concludes this chapter. On Luke 4:16–30 specifically, see the following article and the bibliography gathered therein: Jacques Dupont, "Jésus annonce la bonne nouvelle aux pauvres," *Evangelizare pauperibus: Atti della XXIV Settimana Biblica, Associazione Biblica Italiana* (Brescia: Paideia, 1978) 129–64, 184–87.

34. See Fitzmyer, *Luke* 223.

35. See R. Bultmann, "*aphiēmi, ktl,*" *TDNT* 1.512.

36. This same Greek word occurs in its verbal form (*aphiēmi*) in "forgiveness" passages in the rest of Luke. See 5:20,21,23,24; 7:47,48,49 (recall the use of "creditor" and "debtor" language in 7:40–42); 11:4; 12:10; 17:3,4; 23:34. Note also that the Greek word *aphesis* is used to describe the jubilee of liberation in the Old Testament. See Robert B. Sloan, Jr., *The Favorable Year of the Lord: A Study of Jubilary Theology in the Gospel of Luke* (Austin: Schola, 1977) 118–21.

37. See Fitzmyer, *Luke* 224: "In other words, though Luke often depicts Jesus 'forgiving sins' in the ministry of the Gospel, when he comes to sum up the corresponding effect of Jesus' total work that must be proclaimed, it is stated in terms of his releasing human beings from their debts (= sins) in the sight of God. He has, by all that he was and did, cancelled the debt of guilt incurred by their evil conduct."

38. See our treatment of Luke 13:10–17 below for evidence that God's justice is not just a spiritual reality, but that it has effects in the temporal order. See also Patrick D. Miller, "Luke 4:16–21," *Int* 29 (1975) 417–21.

39. On the death and resurrection imagery present in Luke 4:16–30, see Eugene A. LaVerdiere, *Luke* (New Testament Message 5; Wilmington: Glazier, 1980) 66–68.

40. See Nils A. Dahl, "The Story of Abraham in Luke-Acts," in *Studies in Luke-Acts* 150: "Both stories (13:10–17; 19:1–10) illustrate how God's

promise to Abraham was fulfilled to his children through the ministry of Jesus.''

41. On the theme of women in Luke, see Eugene H. Maly, ''Women and the Gospel of Luke,'' *BTB* 10 (1980) 99–104; Navone, *Themes* 224–29; Ben Witherington III, ''On the Road with Mary Magdalene, Joanna, Susanna, and Other Disciples—Luke 8:1–3,'' *ZNW* 70 (1979) 243–48.

42. The reader should also contrast the behavior of the religious leader in 13:14 with that of the leader in 8:41. These two ''rulers of synagogues'' have different views of Jesus' relationship to the God of life and justice. In Luke's narrative reversal of expectations not all religious leaders are closed to Jesus' revelation of a faithful God.

43. This is the thrust of the thesis of Nuetzel, *Jesus als Offenbarer Gottes*. Unfortunately, he does not embark on a consideration of Luke 23 from this perspective.

44. The linguistic parallels between 18:18 and 14:1; 23:13,35; 24:20 lead me to conclude that ''ruler'' means ''religious leader.'' See also Jacques Dupont, *Les béatitudes, Tome III* 58–59.

45. See note 2 above on almsgiving as the doing of justice. Contrast the justice response of Zacchaeus, a chief tax collector (19:1–10), with that of the religious leader of 18:18–30.

46. On the Lukan theme of God's sovereign grace (*sola gratia*), see Walter Klaiber, ''Eine lukanische Fassung des *sola gratia*: Beobachtungen zu Lk 1,5–56,'' *Rechtfertigung: Festschrift fuer Ernst Kaesemann zum 70. Geburtstag* (ed. J. Friedrich; W. Poehlmann; P. Stuhlmacher; Tuebingen: Mohr; Goettigen: Vandenhoeck & Ruprecht, 1976) 211–18.

47. Luke does not detail the disciples' abandonment of Jesus as Mark does in Mark 14:50.

48. This is the thesis of Dillon's excellent monograph, *Eye-Witnesses*.

49. See Chapter Two above for the model of righteous person as found in Wisdom 2:10–20; 4:20–5:8.

50. See Jesus' teaching about ''love of enemies'' in Luke 6:27–36.

51. See on the theme of peace and justice, Richard J. Cassidy, *Jesus, Politics, and Society: A Study of Luke's Gospel* (Maryknoll: Orbis, 1978); John R. Donahue, ''The Good News of Peace,'' *The Way* 22 (1982) 88–99.

52. See Luise Schottroff, ''Non-Violence and the Love of One's Enemies,'' in L. Schottroff et al., *Essays on the Love Commandment* (Philadelphia: Fortress, 1978) 9–39, esp. 20–28.

53. Jesus freely accepts God's will for him as determined by Isaiah 53:12 which is quoted in Luke 22:37: ''For I tell you that this scripture must be fulfilled in me, 'And he was reckoned with transgressors'; for what is written about me has its fulfillment.''

Excursus On "The Poor" in Luke's Gospel

From 1977 onward study has continued apace on the term, "the poor," as perceived as part of the biblical contrast: "poor and rich." See Bruce C. Birch and Larry L. Rasmussen, *The Predicament of the Prosperous* (Biblical Perspectives on Current Issues; Philadelphia: Westminster, 1978); Jacques Dupont, "The Poor and Poverty in the Gospels and Acts," *Gospel Poverty: Essays in Biblical Theology* (Chicago: Franciscan Herald, 1977) 25–52; Robert J. Karris, "Poor and Rich: The Lukan Sitz im Leben," in *Perspectives on Luke-Acts* (ed. Charles H. Talbert; Macon: Mercer University, 1978) 112–25; L.E. Keck, "Poor," *IBDSup*; George W.E. Nickelsburg, "Riches, The Rich, and God's Judgment in 1 Enoch 92–105 and the Gospel according to Luke," *NTS* 25 (1978/79) 324–44. In this respect, Dupont's conclusion is well worth quoting: "In proclaiming the good news of God's kingdom to the poor, Jesus manifests the care and concern which God has for them, his will to put an end to their suffering. From this proclamation, Christians must hold not that poverty is an ideal but that the poor must be made the object of a completely special love; in this way we share the feelings which God has for them" ("The Poor," 41). This way of looking at biblical poverty has been and can be revolutionary, for it removes poverty from the "weights-and-measures" approach, i.e., my possessions weigh less than theirs and therefore I am poor and they are rich.

Work has begun, and progress has been made in viewing "the poor" from a social and anthropological perspective. See Bruce J. Malina, *The New Testament World: Insights from Cultural Anthropology* (Atlanta: John Knox, 1981) 71–93; Frederick W. Norris, "The Social Status of Early Christianity," *Gospel in Context* 2 (January, 1979) 4–14; Richard L. Rohrbaugh, *The Biblical Interpreter: An Agrarian Bible in an Industrial Age* (Philadelphia: Fortress, 1978). Norris' article will provide a sampling of this approach. He examines all the data and argues well that the communities of primitive Christianity had both rich and poor members. In other words, the commonly held image that most early Christians were slaves and therefore poor is not accurate. This approach raises questions as to how the rich Christians in Luke's communities would have understood passages like Luke 14:33: "So therefore, whoever of you does not renounce all that he has cannot be my disciple.''

Third world theologians have changed the lens by which the same biblical data are being seen. From their perspectives of experienced oppression, they are calling attention to the fact that "poor" in the Bible often means "oppressed." They then ask the question: Who or what is oppressing these people? See Tom Hanks, "Why People Are Poor: What the Bible Says," *Sojourners* 10 (January, 1981) 19–22; Elsa Tamez, *Bible of the Oppressed* (Maryknoll: Orbis, 1982). From this perspective also see Gustavo Gutierrez, *A Theology of Liberation: History, Politics and Salvation* (Maryknoll: Orbis, 1973) 287–306; Julio de Santa Ana, *Good News to the Poor: The Challenge of the Poor in the History of the Church* (Maryknoll: Orbis, 1979).

Still other scholars are reminding interpreters that their own cultures condition the way the texts on "poor and rich" are read. Robert McAfee Brown rightly calls for "hermeneutical circulation": "So it is not just a matter of ourselves and the text, it is a matter of ourselves *and others* and the text. The others are needed to tell us not only how they perceive the text but also how they perceive us perceiving the text (a service we must also perform for them). It is out of this mutual search, mutual interpretation, and mutual correction that we can create a new hermeneutic" (*Theology in a New Key: Responding to Liberation Themes* [Philadelphia: Westminster, 1978] 87–88). See also Klauspeter Blaser, "Christianity, Marxism, and the Poor," *TD* 29 (1981) 217–21; Lee Cormie, "The Hermeneutical Privilege of the Oppressed: Liberation Theologies, Biblical Faith, and Marxist Sociology of Knowledge," *Proceedings of the Catholic Theological Society of America* 33 (1978) 155–81. See now the challenging work by Elisabeth Schuessler Fiorenza, *In Memory of Her: A Feminist Theological Reconstruction of Christian Origins* (New York: Crossroad, 1983). She argues against the normal androcentric reconstruction of Christian origins and states that "in the first century—as today—the majority of the poor and starving were women, especially those women who had no male agencies that might have enabled them to share in the wealth of the patriarchal system" (141).

Chapter Four

THE THEME OF FOOD

In the previous chapter we saw how the theme of justice helped Luke answer the question of how Jesus, God's righteous one and prophet, got himself crucified. In this chapter we will explore the Lukan use of the theme of food to answer the same question.

My major point in this chapter is that in Luke's Gospel Jesus got himself crucified by the way he ate. I will develop that point in three parts. First, I will give a presentation of Luke's pervasive use of the theme of food in his Gospel. In the next two parts I will capture some of the richness of the Lukan motif of food by gathering materials into two bins: in Jesus God demonstrates his fidelity to his hungry creation by feeding it; Jesus is "a glutton and a drunkard."

LUKE'S PERVASIVE USE OF THE MOTIF OF FOOD

There is considerable truth in what one wag said about Luke's Gospel: Jesus is either going to a meal, at a meal, or coming from a meal. The extent, though, of Luke's use of the theme of food is appreciated only when the reader realizes that the aroma of food issues forth from each and every chapter of Luke's Gospel. Food is definitely an important theme and, as such, draws the reader into Luke's faith-inspiring kerygmatic story.[1] It is a theme which, because of its elemental nature, resonates at the depths of our contingent being.[2]

Readers may have some difficulty appreciating this motif. As part of a society which consumes dietbooks by the millions because food is so bounteously available and appetites so rapacious and which has developed its own language and life-style about food—fast-food, convenience-food, junk-food, high-protein food—readers might find it difficult to see through such language screens and reflect upon the pro-

found truths that food is life and that sharing of food is sharing of life.
Readers who are Roman Catholics may have special difficulty in appreciating Luke's use of the motif of food because of a tendency to reduce
almost all occurrences of this motif to eucharistic references. For them
the Benedictine Demetrius R. Dumm provides provocative food for
thought:

> Luke shows a special sensitivity for table-fellowship, not just
> for its own sake but also because it is a sign of a deeper kind
> of hospitality that entertains the strange and alien elements in
> life and looks for good everywhere. This large and generous
> spirit derives from his faith-understanding of the profound
> goodness hidden in the mystery of God.[3]

With our eyes at-the-ready to immerse ourselves in Luke's food symbolism, I will offer a "big picture" view of the occurrences of this
theme in Luke's Gospel and touch upon some of Luke's richly diverse
vocabulary for food. This macro-viewpoint will prime us for our subsequent considerations of two major facets of the Lukan theme of food.
All of these occurrences are leading toward Luke 22–24. Luke's account
of the "Last Supper" (22:14–38) is the last event of "sharing of life" in
a sequence of such events. Jesus, the giver of abundant food for all, is
given vinegar on the cross (23:36); he promises that the crucified evil-
doer will eat of the tree of life in paradise (23:43). Jesus shares the new
life of the resurrection of the just by breaking bread for two disciples
who have abandoned his way of justice (24:30–31,35).

THE "BIG PICTURE" OF THE MOTIF OF FOOD IN
LUKE'S GOSPEL[4]

Before listing the passages in sequence, I want to offer some suggestions to the reader. Readers should try to enter into Luke's rich theme
of food by arranging the materials into patterns for themselves, e.g., Jesus as host; Jesus as guest; outcasts are the hungry.[5] I have tried to express the gist of each passage in a provocative way to entice the reader
to see a familiar passage in a new light. Readers should check each passage for themselves to see whether I have been provocative or obscure.
In any case, the reader should situate the passage in the flow of Luke's

Gospel. The reader might also want to note the various connections between the themes of justice and food.[6] Finally, the reader might want to check the bibliography given in the various footnotes for leads on the diverse dimensions of Luke's food thematic.[7]

Luke 1:15	No strong drink for the prophet of God; see 7:33–34, which contrasts the life-styles of John the Baptist and Jesus on the basis of food and drink.
Luke 1:53	In his justice God will provide the hungry with food; see the beatitude about the hungry in 6:21 and the woe about the full in 6:25.
Luke 2:7,12,16	Jesus in the manger is food for the world.[8]
Luke 2:37	A widow, symbol of dependence on God, fasts.
Luke 3:11	Repentance is shown by an act of justice: sharing food.
Luke 3:17	Repentant are wheat; unrepentant are chaff.
Luke 4:1–4	Jesus fasts as a sign of his dependence upon God for life.[9]
Luke 4:25	God's gracious justice to a pagan widow caught in famine.
Luke 4:39	A person healed by Jesus waits on table (*diakoneō*).
Luke 5:1–11	Peter abandons the food of fish to follow Jesus, the source of true food for life.
Luke 5:29 38	A dispute between Jesus and the religious leaders about his eating habits.
Luke 6:1–5	The sabbath, a day for celebrating life, and the question of eating.
Luke 6:21	God's kingdom justice will provide food for the hungry.
Luke 6:25	The full are given a prophetic warning.
Luke 6:43–46	Good fruit and bad fruit.
Luke 7:31–35	Criticism of the prophets' eating habits: John the Baptist has a demon; Jesus is a glutton and a drunkard.
Luke 7:36–50	A woman recognizes God's justice in Jesus, a son of Wisdom (7:35), and comes for life; the religious leader who invites Jesus to a meal to share life fails to understand the gift of life.

Luke 8:3	Followers of Jesus share life (*diakoneō*) with one another.
Luke 8:11	The word of God as preached by Jesus gives life.[10]
Luke 8:55	Jesus' mercy involves concern that people have something to eat.
Luke 9:3	Those who follow Jesus depend upon God for their sustenance.
Luke 9:10–17	Jesus as giver of abundant life.
Luke 10:2	Harvest as image of mission.
Luke 10:7–8	Sharing of life of food and sharing of the gospel are intimately connected.
Luke 10:38–42	A meal, discipleship, and sharing life (*diakoneō*).[11]
Luke 11:3	Daily bread comes from God.[12]
Luke 11:5–12	Food is sharing of life with friends and children.
Luke 11:27–29	Where is true nourishment: in mother's milk or in the word of God?
Luke 11:37–54	At a meal Jesus criticizes the religious leaders for lack of justice; is sharing life a matter of external hygiene?[13]
Luke 12:1	The teaching and life-style of the religious leaders is leaven.
Luke 12:13–34	Can one trust God to provide life? Can one share life with others by deeds of justice (almsgiving; 12:21,33)?
Luke 12:35–38	Reversal of expectations: the Master serves (*diakoneō*) the servants (*douloi*) at table with food.
Luke 12:41–48	Disciples are to provide food for others.
Luke 13:6–9	Patience with the fig tree, so that it may bear fruit.
Luke 13:18–21	Parables of the kingdom of justice are imaged by growing things.
Luke 13:29–30	The tables are turned at the eschatological table.
Luke 14:1–24	Who comes to dinner? The rich? Or the poor, the maimed, the lame, and the blind?
Luke 14:34–35	Discipleship and salt that works.
Luke 15:1–2	Religious leaders murmur about Jesus' table mates.
Luke 15:11–32	Without its many references to eating = life, the parable of the Prodigal Father is dead.

Luke 16:19–31	Lazarus, a miserable poor wretch, is a child of Abraham, for he has a choice spot at the messianic banquet (16:22).
Luke 17:7–10	In contrast to 12:35–38, servants at table remain servants.
Luke 18:12	Fasting is not used as a sign of dependence upon God by a religious leader.
Luke 19:7	Murmuring about Jesus eating with a chief tax collector, Zacchaeus. See 5:27–32; 15:2.
Luke 20:9–18	Who will share the fruit?
Luke 20:46	Occasions for sharing of life become occasions for self-exaltation.
Luke 21:34	Celebrating life to the point of drunkenness avoids life.
Luke 22:1–38	Jesus does not eat his "last" meal with his family, but with his followers. Jesus' life-style is that of one who serves at table (*diakoneō*).
Luke 23:43	To his dying breath Jesus gives the food of life.
Luke 24:28–35	The giver of life is not dead; he continues to share life. God's kingdom is realized as Jesus eats with his disciples (see 22:18).
Luke 24:41–42	The disciples receive Jesus as a guest, who opens their eyes to see and share life.[14]

In the next paragraphs I will not burden the reader, who may have little or no knowledge of New Testament Greek, with largely incomprehensible detail. Two general points will suffice.

Luke uses a mimimum of forty-five different words to refer to the theme of food, e.g., hunger, harvest, drunkenness. He also uses synonyms for food, some of which are found nowhere else in the New Testament. Here is a sampling:

Luke 9:12	"Provisions" (Greek: *episitismos*)
Luke 9:13	"food" (*brōma*)
Luke 12:23	"food" (*trophē*)
Luke 12:42	"portion of food" (*sitometrion*)
Luke 24:41	"anything to eat" (*brosimos*)

As is readily apparent, Luke is very versatile in his use of food imagery.

In summary, this first part of our study of Luke's use of the language of food has been general in tone. In the next two parts we will bear down on specifics.

IN JESUS GOD DEMONSTRATES HIS FIDELITY TO HIS HUNGRY CREATION BY FEEDING IT

This specific arrangement of Luke's general theme of "food" will deal with the following representative passages: Luke 1:53; 4:1–4; 6:21,25; 8:11–21; 9:10–17.

Luke 1:53

[53]He has filled the hungry with good things, and the rich he has sent empty away.

This verse is part of Luke's Magnificat (1:46–55), which gives an advance interpretation of who Jesus is. In this song God's fulfillment of all that he has planned for creation and humankind is seen as beginning with Jesus' conception.[15] God's plan involves feeding the hungry. The rest of Luke's kerygmatic story will detail how God is faithful to his creation by feeding it through Jesus' ministry of word and mighty deed. I stress "the rest" of the Gospel, for it would seem that on the cross the God who in Jesus fed his hungry creation is unfaithful and not able to give life to his own Son.[16] But God is faithful to his hungry creation, even and especially in the person of his crucified and righteous Son. For as the psalms of the suffering righteous one express it, God's vindication of the righteous takes the form of feeding them to the point of satisfaction. See, e.g., Psalm 22:27: "the needy (*penētes*) shall eat and be satisfied (*emplēsthēsontai*)."[17] Nothing, not even death itself, will stand in the way of God's accomplishment of his purpose and plan. In the Christ event the faithful God feeds all who hunger.

Luke 4:1–4

[1]And Jesus, full of the Holy Spirit, returned from the Jordan, and was led by the Spirit[2] for forty days in the wilderness,

tempted by the devil. And he ate nothing in those days; and when they were ended, he was hungry. ³The devil said to him, 'If you are the Son of God, command this stone to become bread.' ⁴And Jesus answered him, 'It is written, 'Man shall not live by bread alone.''

This passage occurs in a section (3:21–4:13) where Luke is giving his readers greater insight into the significance of Jesus whose Galilean ministry he will begin relating in 4:14–30. A few comments are in order.[18]

Jesus himself, the one in whom God is to feed his hungry creation, fasts. The hungry Jesus is at one with those who are hungry.

In his refusal to succumb to the devil's temptation, Jesus shows his utter confidence in his faithful God who will take care of him and his creation. This Son (3:21–22) also shows his obedience to and trust in his Father's plan of feeding the hungry, a plan which the remainder of Luke's story will reveal.

Joseph Fitzmyer makes the challenging observation that the three temptations of Luke 4:1–13 symbolize the seduction present in the hostility, opposition, and rejection which confronted Jesus constantly throughout his ministry.[19] For our purposes this observation means that Luke 4:1–13 contains advance summaries of the opposition Jesus, the righteous one, will meet at the hands of the religious leaders.[20] In the remainder of Luke's kerygmatic story it will become quite clear that one of Jesus' major temptations dealt with food (4:1–4). Luke's story will describe Jesus as the obedient Son of his Father who serves his Father's food to all by assuming the role of a table servant (22:27) and by shunning a life-style of being waited on hand and foot.[21]

The opening of Luke's passion account in Chapter 22 will narrate the devil's next full-scale attack on Jesus.[22] Significantly, "the opportune time" (4:13) will occur during a holyday and a celebrative meal. The devil's attack will succeed with Judas (22:1–6), who is won over to the life-style of the religious leaders. During this celebrative meal, Jesus' Last Supper, he will warn and encourage his disciples to be faithful to his life-style in giving the food of life to others by being waiters (22:24–27).

Luke 6:21,25

> [21]Blessed are you that hunger now, for you shall be satisfied.
> [25]Woe to you that are full now, for you shall hunger.

Our comments must be necessarily brief on a passage which boasts an extensive bibliography.[23] Luke 6:21,25 occur in Luke's sermon on the plain (6:20–49), which gives a sampling of Jesus' teaching about God's kingly justice and contains a minor refrain about the seriousness of hearing Jesus' word aright (6:27,47).

Luke's kerygmatic story invites the reader to hear the prophet Jesus as he tells that God's promise of a "messianic banquet" is being fulfilled.[24] And as the story line unfolds, that fulfillment of the gift of food to the hungry is not something in the far distant past or future. It is fulfilled now for the reader who hears and believes in Jesus: in Jesus whose "word of God" produces life just as a seed does (see 8:11–21), in Jesus who gives food in abundance to those who hunger in the desert places of life where food seems impossible to find (9:10–17). It is fulfilled now through disciples who help Jesus distribute bread to the hungry (9:16).

In Jesus God is reversing an apparently impossible situation. The evil of hunger does not stand in the way of God's fidelity. He is faithful to his hungry creation which he feeds through Jesus' word, which is actually his own, and through Jesus' gift of plenty.

Luke 8:11–21

> [11]Now the parable is this: The seed is the word of God. [12]The ones along the path are those who have heard; then the devil comes and takes away the word from their hearts, that they may not believe and be saved. [13]And the ones on the rock are those who, when they hear the word, receive it with joy; but these have no root, they believe for a while and in time of temptation fall away. [14]And as for what fell among the thorns, they are those who hear, but as they go on their way they are choked by the cares and riches and pleasures of life, and their fruit does not mature. [15]And as for that in the good soil, they are those who, hearing the word, hold it fast in an honest and good heart, and bring forth fruit with patience. [16]No one after

lighting a lamp covers it with a vessel, or puts it under a bed, but puts it on a stand, that those who enter may see the light. [17]For nothing is hid that shall not be made manifest, nor anything secret that shall not be known and come to light. [18]Take heed then how you hear; for to him who has will more be given, and from him who has not, even what he thinks that he has will be taken away. [19]Then his mother and his brethren came to him, but they could not reach him for the crowd. [20]And he was told, 'Your mother and your brethren are standing outside, desiring to see you.' [21]But he said to them, 'My mother and my brethren are those who hear the word of God and do it.'

This passage also occurs in Luke's account of Jesus' Galilean ministry. It is set in a context of Jesus "preaching and bringing the good news of the kingdom of God" (8:1) and underscores "hearing."[25]

Luke identifies the "seed" with "the word of God" (8:11; see also 5:1; 8:21; 11:28 on "the word of God"). Although the Lukan interpretation of the parable of the sower (8:11–15) accentuates the types of soil which receive the word/seed, the "food" aspect of the "seed" is still present. The seed gives life, especially when allowed to mature within the listeners (8:15). As a matter of fact, the nature of the seed is to give the life which is salvation (8:12). This "word of God" which gives life is sown in Jesus' preaching and teaching.[26]

Those who have ears to hear should hear (see 8:8). As in the previous block of teaching we examined above (6:20–49), the reader is challenged to listen to and understand the word of God as preached by Jesus.[27] We can take this "listening" motif a step further. Raymond E. Brown is of the opinion that Luke 8:19–21 (along with 11:27–29) is the basis for Luke's presentation of Mary in his infancy narrative.[28] Mary is the model disciple, the one who is made alive by hearing and responding to God's word.[29] Further, there is an element of "intersignification" between Mary as the ideal disciple who is fed by God's word and Mary the humiliated one (1:48) who must turn to God for justice. "Luke presents Mary as a disciple not only because she said, 'Be it done unto me according to your word,' but because she understood what the word meant in terms of the life of the poor and the slaves of whom she was a representative."[30]

Luke 9:10–17

> [10]On their return the apostles told him what they had done.
> And he took them and withdrew apart to a city called Beth-
> saida. [11]When the crowds learned it, they followed him; and
> he welcomed them and spoke to them of the kingdom of God,
> and cured those who had need of healing. [12]Now the day began
> to wear away; and the twelve came and said to him, 'Send the
> crowd away, to go into the villages and country round about,
> to lodge and get provisions; for we are here in a lonely place.'
> [13]But he said to them, 'You give them something to eat.' They
> said, 'We have no more than five loaves and two fish—unless
> we are to go and buy food for all these people.' [14]For there
> were about five thousand men. And he said to his disciples,
> 'Make them sit down in companies, about fifty each.' [15]And
> they did so, and made them all sit down. [16]And taking the five
> loaves and the two fish he looked up to heaven, and blessed
> and broke them, and gave them to the disciples to set before
> the crowd. [17]And all ate and were satisfied. And they took up
> what was left over, twelve baskets of broken pieces.

What was presented in beatitude form earlier in Luke 6:21 is narrated
dramatically in this story: those who hunger are satisfied in the kingly
ministry of Jesus. At the end of Luke's presentation of Jesus' Galilean
ministry, those in a ''desert place'' (9:12)[31] are given so much food that
they are satisfied and there are leftovers aplenty (9:17). In Jesus God has
truly fulfilled his promise of feeding his creation.[32]

And as Luke 9:11 makes quite clear, Jesus' fulfillment of God's
promises of giving food to his needy creation is linked to his preaching
of the kingdom of God. A hungry creation mocks God's kingly justice.
Jesus' kingly justice not only involves extending God's mercy to the
poor,[33] but also embraces those who in their hunger cry out for God's
justice. And Luke 9:15 shows that disciples are to be involved in this
justice ministry of feeding the hungry.

This story of God's bounteous gift of life to his creation in Jesus is
followed by Luke's first prediction of Jesus' passion and vindication
(9:22). The cross is on the horizon. Human selfishness, represented by
the religious leaders mentioned in 9:22, will not tolerate such largess of

food.[34] They will plot the demise of the giver of life, but God will thwart their plans. The faithful God will resurrect Jesus who will be recognized when he again breaks the bread of life (24:28–31,35). And disciples who have been beneficiaries of their Master's bounty are instructed about carrying their cross daily after Jesus (9:23). "In Lk's mind, *the Master breaking bread with his followers is the Master sharing his mission and destiny with them!*"[35]

Luke's kerygmatic story presents the reader with Jesus, the righteous one and preacher of God's good news to the poor, who by his words and mighty deeds embodies a God who deeply and graciously cares for and feeds his hungry creation. This is the faithful God of Jesus.

JESUS IS A GLUTTON AND A DRUNKARD

Another specific way of arranging the Lukan materials on the theme of food is to use the proverbial "a glutton and a drunkard" of Luke 7:34 as a focal point. Applied to Jesus, this proverb means that Jesus got himself crucified because he ate with apostates from true religion.

We will examine three representative passages: Luke 7:34 which speaks of the religious leaders' criticism of Jesus' eating habits; Luke 14:1–24 which deals with Jesus' criticism of the eating habits of the religious leaders; Luke 22:14–38 which is Jesus' farewell instructions to his disciples on how they are to eat after his death, in memory of him. I would advise readers to be on the outlook especially for the "together with" and "separation from" aspects of Jesus' meals.

Luke 7:34

> [34]The Son of man has come eating and drinking; and you say, 'Behold, a glutton and a drunkard, a friend of tax collectors and sinners!'

This verse is important for Luke's presentation of Jesus during the Galilean phase of his kingly ministry. A number of observations will bring out its importance.

The phrase, "a glutton and a drunkard," is proverbial for an apostate and is based on Deuteronomy 21:18–21:[36]

> [18]If a man has a stubborn and rebellious son, who will not obey the voice of his father or the voice of his mother, and, though they chastise him, will not give heed to them, [19]then his father and his mother shall take hold of him and bring him out to the elders of his city at the gate of the place where he lives, [20]and they shall say to the elders of his city, 'This our son is stubborn and rebellious, he will not obey our voice; he is a glutton and a drunkard.' [21]Then all the men of the city shall stone him to death with stones; so you shall purge the evil from your midst; and all Israel shall hear, and fear.

Jesus' apostasy is eating with tax collectors[37] and sinners—social and religious outcasts, people regarded as apostates by the standards of the religious leaders.[38]

When we link the Lukan Jesus' eating habits with his proclamation of God's kingly justice, we begin to spot another aspect of the importance of Luke 7:34. By eating with outcasts, Jesus is saying in dramatic form that God shares life together with them. His eating and drinking with sinners and tax collectors is an "acted parable" of God's kingly justice.[39] In the Lukan Jesus' kingly ministry God shares food with all, even those considered "non-elect." Joachim Jeremias captures much of the meaning of the Lukan "acted parable":

> In the East, even today, to invite a man to a meal was an honor. It was an offer of peace, trust, brotherhood, and forgiveness; in short, sharing a table meant sharing life. In Judaism in particular, table-fellowship means fellowship before God, for the eating of a piece of broken bread by everyone who shares in a meal brings out the fact that they all have a share in the blessing which the master of the house had spoken over the unbroken bread. Thus Jesus' meals with the publicans and sinners, too, are not only events on a social level, not only an expression of his unusual humanity and social generosity and his sympathy with those who were despised, but had an even deeper significance. They are an expression of the mission and message of Jesus (Mk 2:17), eschatological meals, anticipatory celebrations of the feast in the end-time (Lk 13:28f; Mt 8:11–12), in which the community of the saints is

already being represented (Mk 2:19). The inclusion of sinners in the community of salvation, achieved in table-fellowship, is the most meaningful expression of the message of the redeeming love of God.[40]

Jeremias' points are generally very well taken. But as we have implied from time to time earlier, Luke's thematic symbolism should not be restricted to a particular locality or ethnic group. Thus, his food thematic is universal, transcending the culture of the East and of the Jews. Luke's kerygmatic story of Jesus' eating with social and religious outcasts resonates with all readers in whose cultures sharing food is sharing life.

A final observation on the importance of Luke 7:34 is in order. In Luke 7:34 the "you" of "you say" refers to the religious leaders. My argument for this position is based on the context. In 7:29–30 Luke clearly separates out "all the people and the tax collectors" from the religious leaders. It is the religious leaders who criticize both John the Baptist (see the "you say" of 7:33) and Jesus for the way they eat. As I. Howard Marshall says of Luke 7:34: "Once again the Jewish leaders failed to see the significance of the living parable in the One who brought to sinners the offer of divine forgiveness and friendship."[41]

In Luke's kerygmatic story the religious leaders criticize Jesus not only because of his table companions, but also because he does not instruct his disciples to fast (5:27–39; see 18:9–14). The Lukan Jesus' restrictions on fasting go hand in glove with his happy table fellowship with outcasts. As Joseph Wimmer says so insightfully, Jesus dispensed from fasting

not in order to eat, drink, and be merry, but in order to share a fellowship of love and conviviality with tax collectors and sinners, with the outcast and rejected, those most starving for love and acceptance and yet most deprived of it. The contrast between the fasting Pharisees who fear to touch a tax collector lest they become unclean, and Jesus, who calls Levi to be an apostle and who pleasantly dines in the company of sinners, is striking.[42]

In sum, in the "acted parable" of his joyous table fellowship with outcasts, Jesus shows a faithful God's universal love and mercy. To the religious leaders Jesus' promiscuous table fellowship is apostasy and an act of perverting the people (see 23:2,5,14). Jesus, a glutton and a drunkard, will die for the way he eats.

Luke 14:1–24

> ¹One sabbath when he went to eat bread at the house of a ruler who belonged to the Pharisees, they were watching him. ²And behold, there was a man before him who had dropsy. ³And Jesus spoke to the lawyers and Pharisees, saying, 'Is it lawful to heal on the sabbath, or not?' ⁴But they were silent. Then he took him and healed him, and let him go. ⁵And he said to them, 'Which of you, having an ass or an ox that has fallen into a well, will not immediately pull him out on a sabbath day?' ⁶And they could not reply to this. ⁷Now he told a parable to those who were invited, when he marked how they chose the places of honor, saying to them, ⁸'When you are invited by any one to a marriage feast, do not sit down in a place of honor, lest a more eminent man than you be invited by him; ⁹and he who invited you both will come and say to you, 'Give place to this man,' and then you will begin with shame to take the lowest place. ¹⁰But when you are invited, go and sit in the lowest place, so that when your host comes he may say to you, 'Friend, go up higher'; then you will be honored in the presence of all who sit at table with you. ¹¹For every one who exalts himself will be humbled, and he who humbles himself will be exalted.' ¹²He said also to the man who had invited him, 'When you give a dinner or a banquet, do not invite your friends or your brothers or your kinsmen or rich neighbors, lest they also invite you in return, and you be repaid. ¹³But when you give a feast, invite the poor, the maimed, the lame, the blind, ¹⁴and you will be blessed, because they cannot repay you. You will be repaid at the resurrection of the just.' ¹⁵When one of those who sat at table with him heard this, he said to him, 'Blessed is he who shall eat bread in the kingdom of God!' ¹⁶But he said to him, 'A man once gave a great banquet, and invited many; ¹⁷and at the time for the banquet he sent his servant to say to those who had been invited, 'Come; for all is

now ready.' [18]But they all alike began to make excuses. The first said to him, 'I have bought a field, and I must go out and see it; I pray you, have me excused.' [19]And another said, 'I have bought five yoke of oxen, and I go to examine them; I pray you, have me excused.' [20]And another said, 'I have married a wife, and therefore I cannot come.' [21]So the servant came and reported this to his master. Then the householder in anger said to his servant, 'Go out quickly to the streets and lanes of the city, and bring in the poor and maimed and blind and lame.' [22]And the servant said, 'Sir, what you commanded has been done, and still there is room.' [23]And the master said to the servant, 'Go out to the highways and hedges, and compel people to come in, that my house may be filled. [24]For I tell you, none of those men who were invited shall taste my banquet.'

This representative text comes from Luke's account of Jesus' journey to his Father (9:51–19:44) wherein he describes Jesus as calling the crowds to follow him, giving his disciples further instructions about the meaning of his justice way of life, and disputing with the religious leaders. After giving some general Jewish and Graeco-Roman background about the imagery of our passage, I will make specific observations about Jesus' criticism of the way the religious leaders ate. My main point in this section is: Jesus reveals a God who "eats with," shares life with society's handicapped and declares a person righteous who does the same.

James A. Sanders has helped us appreciate the Jewish background of Luke 14.1–24, especially 14:13,21: the poor, the maimed, the lame and the blind.[43] His investigation of those forbidden access to meals in Jewish society is very illuminative. As I list these individuals, I would ask the reader to compare this list with those individuals mentioned in Luke 14:13,21.

The sons of Aaron who are forbidden to offer the bread of God are: blind, lame, mutilated face, limb too long, injured foot, injured hand, hunchback, dwarf, defect in sight, itching disease, scabs, crushed testicles, any blemish (see Lev 21:17–23). The covenanters at Qumran, near the Dead Sea, listed the following folk as those forbidden entry to the messianic banquet: afflicted in flesh, crushed in feet or hands, lame, blind, deaf, dumb, defective eyesight, senility (1 QSa ii 5–22). The

Qumran monks also forbade the following a share in the last holy war: women and boys, lame, blind, halt, permanent defect in flesh, afflicted with impurity of flesh, impure sexual organs (1 QM vii 4–6).[44] Luke seems to have been responsible for adding "the poor" to the list of pariahs in Luke 14:13,21.

There is some evidence that not only Jewish society, but also Graeco-Roman society had a bias against the handicapped. As W. den Boer writes:

> In Greece the state took upon itself the care of those members of the community who had been maimed in battle. It is to its everlasting honour that the Greek state did not allow those who had served their country with life and limb to waste away in misery. This rule, as I see it, deserves all the more praise, when we consider that other maimed or otherwise deformed persons were more likely to be treated with hostility by the community.[45]

From the evidence adduced above from the Jewish and non-Jewish sources, I would universalize "the maimed, the lame, and the blind" of Luke 14:13,21 to mean the handicapped of society. These individuals are representative of those people whom a society would deem to be outside the pale of its care and concern.

Luke draws upon Greek imagery in setting 14:1–24 in the Graeco-Roman symposium pattern.[46] During the flow of the symposium of 14:1–24 the topic of "places of honor" occurs in 14:7–11. This motif occurs frequently in the literature about symposia.[47] Lucian's *Convivium* 8–9 offers a comic elaboration on this motif:

> By that time we had to take our places, for almost everyone was there. On the right as you enter, the women occupied the whole couch, as there were a good many of them, with the bride among them, very scrupulously veiled and hedged in by the women. Toward the back door came the rest of the company according to the esteem in which each was held. Opposite the women, the first was Eucritus, and then Aristaenetus. Then a question was raised whether Zenothemis the Stoic should have precedence, he being an old man, or Hermon the

Epicurean, because he was a priest of the Twin Brethren and a member of the leading family in the city. But Zenothemis solved the problem; 'Aristaenetus,' said he, 'if you put me second to this man here,—an Epicurean, to say nothing worse of him,—I shall go away and leave you in full possession of your board. . . .'[48]

The general background material I have given above about prejudices against handicapped persons and seeking after first places at feasts will help us appreciate certain key points about Luke 14:1–24. In 14:7–11 Jesus criticizes the religious leaders for the way they eat. In seeking after places of honor, they are using a meal which celebrates God's gift of food and life as a means of celebrating themselves. Implicitly, Jesus, the prophet of God's good news to the poor, is criticizing the religious leaders for not being "waiters" as he himself is, the one who serves the Father's good food to all.[49] In Luke 20:46 Jesus will again criticize the religious leaders for seeking after places of honor at feasts.

In Chapter Three we discussed the life-style of the "righteous" person. Luke 14:12–14 makes the clear and forceful point that the "righteous" person, the one who will be repaid at the "resurrection of the just," is the person who shares food with the disadvantaged. And sharing food is the symbol for sharing life.

The parable in Luke 14:15–24 ties all of 14:1–24 together. "To eat bread in the kingdom of God" (14:15) repeats the "to eat bread" which began this section (14:1).[50] The gathering of the religious leaders "to eat bread" together is for them an "acted parable" of the nature of the messianic banquet. Their closed table fellowship reveals those whom God has elected and those whom he has rejected.[51] As Charles W. F. Smith says so pointedly: "It is, then, in reply to this attitude (smug self-confidence) that Luke represents the parable as being spoken, as if Jesus had turned to his sanctimonious neighbor and said, 'Yes, but let me tell you a story.' In this context it is not merely effective but well-nigh devastating."[52] As we have seen earlier in this chapter, the true "acted parable" of God's messianic banquet is Jesus' table fellowship together with sinners and tax collectors.

The final point about Luke 14:15–24 is its reversal theme: the expected ones, the elect,[53] do not respond to Jesus' invitation,[54] but the unexpected ones do heed it. For this last point to make full sense, one must remember that the "poor and maimed and blind and lame" of 14:21 and the "homeless"[55] of 14:22 are not forced against their wills to come to the banquet. The "compel" of 14:23 reflects oriental hospitality.[56] The handicapped know their need, are open to the faithful God's call in Jesus, and come freely to his banquet of life. Apparent injustice on God's part for their condition has not closed down their search for him and his gift of life.[57]

In the light of the criticism of 11:37–54 and now of 14:1–24 it is no wonder that the hostility of the religious leaders mounts against Jesus. After Jesus' last criticism of how the religious leaders eat (20:46), they will plot his murder (22:1–2).

Luke 22:14–38

[14]And when the hour came, he sat at table, and the apostles with him. [15]And he said to them, 'I have earnestly desired to eat this passover with you before I suffer; [16]for I tell you I shall not eat it until it is fulfilled in the kingdom of God.' [17]And he took a cup, and when he had given thanks he said, 'Take this, and divide it among yourselves; [18]for I tell you that from now on I shall not drink of the fruit of the vine until the kingdom of God comes.' [19]And he took bread, and when he had given thanks he broke it and gave it to them, saying, 'This is my body which is given for you. Do this in remembrance of me.' [20]And likewise the cup after supper, saying, 'This cup which is poured out for you is the new covenant in my blood. [21]But behold the hand of him who betrays me is with me on the table. [22]For the Son of man goes as it has been determined; but woe to that man by whom he is betrayed!' [23]And they began to question one another, which of them it was that would do this. [24]A dispute also arose among them, which of them was to be regarded as the greatest. [25]And he said to them, 'The kings of the Gentiles exercise lordship over them; and those in authority over them are called benefactors. [26]But not so with you; rather let the greatest among you become as the youngest, and the leader as one who serves. [27]For which is the greater, one who sits at table, or one who serves? Is it not the one who sits at table? But I am among you as one who serves. [28]You are

those who have continued with me in my trials; ²⁹as my Father appointed a kingdom for me, so do I appoint for you ³⁰that you may eat and drink at my table in my kingdom, and sit on thrones judging the twelve tribes of Israel. ³¹Simon, Simon, behold, Satan demanded to have you, that he might sift you like wheat, ³²but I have prayed for you that your faith may not fail; and when you have turned again, strengthen your brethren.' ³³And he said to him, 'Lord, I am ready to go with you to prison and to death.' ³⁴He said, 'I tell you, Peter, the cock will not crow this day, until you three times deny that you know me.' ³⁵And he said to them, 'When I sent you out with no purse or bag or sandals, did you lack anything?' They said, 'Nothing.' ³⁶He said to them, 'But now, let him who has a purse take it, and likewise a bag. And let him who has no sword sell his mantle and buy one. ³⁷For I tell you that this scripture must be fulfilled in me, ''And he was reckoned with transgressors''; for what is written about me has its fulfilment.' ³⁸And they said, 'Look, Lord, here are two swords.' And he said to them, 'It is enough.'

This passage is so rich that it is impossible to capture all of its meaning in the compass of this book. My goal is to set some of the elements of its food symbolism ''in motion once more'' for the reader. After giving some general perspectives on Luke's gathering together of themes in 22:14–38, I will provide specific explorations on Jesus' fidelity and on the disciples' encouragement.

PERSPECTIVES

Luke's general perspectives could be summarized in the following sentences. Luke 22:14–38 is Jesus' farewell discourse at his last meal. This meal's center of attention is not Jesus' words of institution in 22:19b–20. This meal is a last supper in a sequence of meals celebrated by Jesus, ''a glutton and a drunkard.'' During this meal God's promises are fulfilled. Throughout the length and breadth of 22:14–38 Luke exhorts his readers. These brief sentences are spelled out in the following paragraphs.

Luke has formed this material into a farewell discourse in which Jesus, like worthies of old, speaks about the meaning of life and tells his disciples how to live life.[58] An example of this literary form is found in "The Testament of Joseph" in the intertestamental book called *The Testaments of the Twelve Patriarchs*.[59] Joseph is about to die and calls his children and relatives to him. His life of fidelity to God becomes a model for them as Joseph tells of his chastity in the face of the temptations of Pharaoh's wife and of his conciliatory love toward his brothers who had sold him into slavery. The one who seemed doomed to death and separated from his people is rescued by God and becomes the savior of his people. Through his story of Joseph the author exhorts his readers to similar fidelity to God in the midst of adversity.[60] As we will see below, Jesus bequeaths to his disciples a life-style of fidelity to a Father who wants them to help effect his kingly justice of feeding those in need.

This meal is a "last" supper in a sequence of "suppers" in Luke. Check back over Luke 5:27–32, where Jesus ate with Levi and other sinners whom Levi, turned repentant and missionary, had called to follow Jesus. Such table fellowship was an "acted parable" of God's universal love. Recall Luke 7:36–50 which narrates Jesus the prophet at a meal in the house of a religious leader. Jesus lives out his teaching about the forgiveness of sins. In Luke 9:10–17 Jesus provides an abundant feast for those in a desert place. The Martha-Mary story of Luke 10:38–42 reveals that Jesus, contrary to the rabbis, calls women to follow him and to serve God's needy creation. Luke 11:37–54 presents Jesus at table with religious leaders, prophetically challenging them for their lack of justice. Luke 14:1–24 again features Jesus at table with religious leaders; Jesus critiques their way of eating and exhorts them to care for the disadvantaged and not for self. Luke 19:1–10 is the high point of Jesus' table association with tax collectors. Despite the murmuring of the bystanders, Jesus purposes to stay and dine with Zacchaeus, a chief tax collector, whose justice work consists in giving half of his possessions to the poor. Indeed, Jesus is "a glutton and a drunkard." The reader should note how many features of these previous meals come together in the farewell meal of Luke 22:14–38, e.g., controversy.

Jesus' predictions of his passion and vindication are being fulfilled in this passage. See Luke 9:22; 9:43b–45; 18:31–34. Indeed, a prophet cannot die outside of Jerusalem (see 13:31–35).[61]

The reader's eyes may have been trained by liturgical usage to pay greatest attention to the words of institution in Luke 22:19–20.[62] Scholars like Paul Minear rightly caution against this: "In this story the center of gravity lies not in the words of institution but, as at earlier tables, in the four key dialogues between Jesus and the disciples."[63] Since Luke 22:14–38 is a unit, no part, not even 22:19–20, should be isolated from the whole which provides its interpretative background.

The text is directed to the readers. Its intent is kerygmatic, to offer proclamation and not historical detail. Its masterful use of food symbolism is meant to draw the readers into the meaning of the supper for their lives. Readers are not to be passive spectators of historical events. For example, Luke 22:21–23 does not mention Judas by name. Luke has moved beyond the particulars to the universal. Readers, who have been invited by Luke's kerygmatic story time after time to assume the justice life-style of Jesus, can see themselves as the one questioned at a meal which celebrates that life-style.[64]

Finally, Luke's perspective is that of fulfillment of promise. Jesus, God's righteous one and God's prophet of good news to the poor, is described as looking beyond the cross to his endowment with kingly power (22:29–30).[65] The God in whom he trusted as the faithful God has already, in an anticipatory exercise of his justice, given the life of the resurrection of the just (14:14–15) to his righteous one.

JESUS' COMMITMENT TO HIS FAITHFUL GOD

This segment of Luke's kerygmatic narrative leaves no doubt that Jesus, whose life of fidelity was seen in advance in the temple scene of 2:49 and in the temptation scene of 4:1–4, is faithful to his Father, even to his death. Jesus, who had in his kingly ministry been servant of God's food to all people, is faithful to God to the end. As he prepares to suffer, he offers his disciples food. That is the meaning of Jesus' gift of the cup in 22:17. And Jesus' fidelity to God continues after his death. For he exercises God's kingly rule of feeding the hungry after his exaltation (see Luke 24:30,43; Acts 1:4; 10:41). And in eating with his disciples, the risen Jesus shows that God's kingdom has come (22:16,18).

Luke 22:19–20 provides a similar, but different view of the "last" meal. Jesus' life of serving food to outcasts and apostates earned him the reputation of being "a glutton and a drunkard." His criticisms of the religious leaders' way of eating issued in their plot to kill him. On the eve of his suffering, Jesus' entire life (body and blood), a life for others to the point of death, is bread and wine for his disciples. Jesus' life gives meaning to their lives. A meal in memory of Jesus is one which celebrates and prolongs his life-style of justice and of serving the Father's food to all.

On one level it is not true that Jesus, who is depicted as reclining throughout the meal recounted in 22:14–38, is serving at table (22:27). But on another—on a more profound, thematic and theological level—it is surpassingly true that Jesus is among his disciples as a waiter. In serving God's food to others, Jesus embodies God's kingly justice. Waiting on table is Jesus' life-style and has been contrasted earlier in Luke's story with that of the religious leaders, who seek places of honor at table (14:7; 20:46) and with that of the rich fool and Dives who feast sumptuously without a care for sharing food with others through almsgiving (see 12:13–21 and 16:19–31).

Twice our passage uses Jesus' obedience to God's will as found in Scripture as a means of showing his fidelity to his Father (22:22,37). The stakes of his commitment are the highest possible—life and death. For to remain committed to the Father is to be in conflict with Satan (22:53). Who is in control of food and of life? Is it the faithful God who is directing his prophet Jesus to continue to give people food and drink even though it seems that this director cannot even sustain his prophet? Or is it Satan, who has returned at this "opportune time" (see 4:13), to shake Jesus' disciples vigorously in hopes that their faith in the faithful God of Jesus will fail (22:31–34)?

Ever since 4:1–13 Luke has painted a picture of Jesus as a person of integrity, obedient to his Father's will. From Luke 22:14–38 onward Jesus' probity and loving obedience are found in almost every verse. These twin themes will hit their literary and theological high point in Chapter 23.

ENCOURAGEMENT FOR THE DISCIPLES

As we have just seen, Luke 22:14–38 underscores Jesus' life-style of trust in his Father and commitment to his kingly justice of feeding the hungry despite the accusation that he is a glutton and a drunkard. Luke presents Jesus' disciples, not his family, at table with him and sets them over against the faithful Jesus. They are strengthened by him, but they also will stumble.

The disciples are to eat as Jesus ate, in memory of him (22:19). Their continual sharing of food with one another in memory of Jesus' table fellowship is their commitment to Jesus' kingly justice of feeding the hungry and eating with outcasts although such commitment might result in persecution. And this meal, placed in a farewell discourse setting, has a dual future orientation. It looks beyond the crucifixion to the resurrection: by giving his crucified righteous one and prophet the life of the resurrection, the Father has dramatized his faithfulness to his promises of feeding a hungry creation and shown what his kingdom really means. As the disciples eat in Jesus' memory, they trust in the faithful God who has fed his creation in Jesus, is feeding it now in this meal, and will give it definitive life when his kingdom is completely realized.[66]

Disciples are challenged by Luke 22:21–23 to examine their life-styles at a meal which celebrates Jesus' life-style of giving food to others. Might their lives be the opposite of what is celebrated at this meal?

The religious leaders have provided negative examples of those who seek after the first places at celebrations of life (14:7 and 20:46). The disciples are drilled with Jesus' positive example of one who serves God's food to others to the point of giving his life for the life of others (22:24–27).

Despite the apparent infidelity expressed in their seeking after greatness (22:24–27), the disciples are defined in 22:28 as those who have faithfully stood by Jesus in his persecutions,[67] persecutions to leave the Father's way and to join ranks with the religious leaders and their life-style of injustice and feeding of self. Jesus' care for his disciples is so deep that Satan and persecutions cannot wrest them from his hands (22:31–34).[68]

Luke 22:35–38 is not as clear in all respects as one might like, but its main point is clear. As the disciples continue Jesus' mission of feeding others, they are not going to be freed from persecutions and strife. They, too, may be called gluttons and drunkards. The metaphor of "swords" points to this violence. And as 22:47–53 will narrate, to understand "swords" literalistically is to misunderstand the peaceful Jesus.[69]

In Luke 22:14–38 the disciples are often contrasted unfavorably with Jesus: they jockey for positions of honor; they lack integrity. Paul Minear does not overinterpret the evidence too much when he notes that in 22:14–38 Luke describes Jesus as being among transgressors.[70] And the transgressors are not now the unconverted tax collectors and sinners, but his own disciples. Just as earlier meals had celebrated God's forgiveness, so too does this one. Being with Jesus at table provides life-giving forgiveness to disciples to become more faithful waiters to those who hunger for life.

CONCLUSION TO CHAPTER FOUR

In this chapter Luke's theme of food has helped us answer the question of how Jesus got to the cross. Jesus got himself crucified because of the way he ate. The religious leaders could not tolerate this prophet of good news to the poor who not only in word, but especially at meals criticized their way of life. They also termed him "a glutton and a drunkard," for his way of eating did not accord with their view of divine concourse. Jesus was, for them, a spokesperson for an alien God. As they will declare before Pilate, Jesus was leading the people astray.

And why does Luke's kerygmatic story depict Jesus as enjoying life so much? Luke's view of God is the answer. And as his narrative goes, Jesus is the revealer of this God, the faithful God who feeds his hungry creation, rectifies the ills that plague it, and rejoices to sup with sinners. Can the reader believe in this God?

Our consideration of Luke 22 at the end of this chapter has prepared us for Luke's description of Jesus' last hours in Jerusalem. The Book of Wisdom offers an excellent advance commentary. Wisdom 2:19–20 bears eloquent testimony to Jesus' passion as God's righteous one: "Let us test him with insult and torture, that we may find out how gentle he is, and make trial of his forebearance. Let us condemn him to a shameful death, for, according to what he says, he will be protected." In the face of such insult, Jesus maintains his moral integrity and is protected by his faithful God.

And Wisdom 5:4–6 records what the oppressors of the righteous one say when they see how God has vindicated him: " 'This is the man whom we once held in derision and made a byword of reproach—we fools! We thought his life was madness and that his end was without honor. Why has he been numbered among the sons of God? And why is his lot among the saints? So it was we who strayed from the way of truth, and the light of righteousness did not shine on us.' "

NOTES

1. See Chapter One above on the reader's role in co-creating the text, esp. Robertson, "Literature, the Bible as," *IDBSup* 549 and Ricoeur, *Interpretation Theory* 75.

2. See James P. Mackey, *Jesus The Man and The Myth* (New York: Paulist, 1979) 77–82.

3. "Luke 24:44–49 and Hospitality" in *Sin, Salvation, and the Spirit* 238.

4. This "big picture" is not meant to be an exhaustive listing. Earlier studies on this thematic include the following: E.C. Davis, "The Significance of the Shared Meal in Luke-Acts" (Ann Arbor: Xerox University Microfilms, 1967). This doctoral dissertation from Southern Baptist Theological Seminary focuses on the messianic banquet aspect of the "shared meal." See also Paul S. Minear, "Some Glimpses of Luke's Sacramental Theology," *Worship* 44 (1970) 322–31; John Navone, *Themes* 11–37; Joachim Wanke, *Beobachtungen zum Eucharistieverstaendnis des Lukas auf Grund der lukanischen Mahlberichte* (Erfurter Theologische Schriften 8; Leipzig: St. Benno, 1973). It should be remarked that these studies take the Lukan references to "table fellowship" as their key to Luke's use of the theme of food. While this approach has been very helpful in the past, I am arguing here that a broader approach will open up more of the riches of Luke's understanding of the faithful God.

5. Luke's use of the theme of food is so profound that it cannot be programmed. What J. Hillis Miller says of poets is true of evangelists, especially of Luke: "Though each poet is different, each contains his own form of undecidability. This might be defined by saying that the critic can never show decisively whether or not the work of the writer is 'decidable,' whether or not it is capable of being definitively interpreted. The critic cannot unscramble the tangle of lines of meaning, comb its threads out so they shine clearly side by side. He can only retrace the text, set its elements in motion once more . . . " ("The Critic as Host," *Deconstruction and Criticism* [New York: Seabury, 1979] 248). My goal in this chapter is to set the Lukan "elements" of food symbolsim "in motion once more" for my readers.

6. See the Introduction above and the reference there to Ricoeur's notion of "intersignification." In my listing of the "food" passages below I will point out many of the interconnections between the two themes of food and justice.

7. In my formulation of the "big picture" of Luke's motif of food, I have been influenced by Gillian Feeley-Harnik, *The Lord's Table: Eucharist and Passover in Early Christianity* (Symbol and Culture: Philadelphia: University of Pennsylvania, 1981). On p. 72 she writes: " . . . food, articulated in terms of who eats what with whom under which circumstances, had long been one of the

most important languages in which Jews conceived and conducted special relations among human beings and between human beings and God . . . : 1) The power of the Lord is manifested in his ability to control food; to feed is to bless, to confer life; to feed bad food or to starve is to judge or punish, to confer death. 2) Acceptance of the power and authority of the Lord is symbolized by acceptance of his food. 3) Rejection of the power and authority of the Lord is symbolized by seeking after food he has forbidden. 4) People 'limit' or 'tempt' the Lord—that is, question the extent of his power or authority—by questioning his ability to feed them. 5) The Lord's word is equated with food. 6) Eating joins people with the Lord or separates them.'' The approach of Feeley-Harnik, which is quite beneficial, needs to be expanded by considerations of almsgiving, jubilee, and Deut 15:4 (as reflected in Acts 4:34). Then, her approach would be strengthened and in a solid position to answer objections raised by Lukan liberation theologians, e.g., does God or do first world countries control food? For another anthropological approach to food, see Mary Douglas and Baron Isherwood, *The World of Goods* (New York: Basic Books, 1979) 66–70, 204–05.

8. See Raymond E. Brown, *The Birth of the Messiah: A Commentary on the Infancy Narratives in Matthew and Luke* (Garden City: Doubleday, 1977) 420: ''Jesus is born in the city of David, not in lodgings like an alien, but in a manger where God sustains his people.'' See also my *Invitation to Luke* 48: ''Jesus, who lies in a feeding trough, is food for the world.''

9. On this passage and other Lukan passages which deal with fasting, see the excellent monograph by Joseph F. Wimmer, *Fasting in the New Testament: A Study in Biblical Theology* (Theological Inquiries; New York: Paulist, 1982).

10. The reader is invited to check the other references to ''word of God'' in Luke's Gospel, 5:1; 8:21; 11:28, to see some of the interconnections between Jesus' word and God's gift of food. For the significance of this theme in Acts, see Jerome Kodell, '' 'The Word of God Grew': The Ecclesial Tendency of *Logos* in Acts 6,7; 12,24; 19,20,'' *Bib* 55 (1974) 505–19.

11. For a literary-critical appreciation of this passage, see Eugcnc LaVerdiere, *New Testament in the Life of the Church: Evangelization, Catechetics, Prayer, Homiletics* (Notre Dame: Ave Maria, 1980) 100–06.

12. See Peter Edmonds, ''The Lucan Our Father: A Summary of Luke's Teaching on Prayer?'' *ExpT* 91 (1980) 140–43, esp. pp. 141–42 where Edmonds rightly relates the gift of bread (11:3) to the gift of the Holy Spirit (11:13). He writes: ''A prayer for material bread is thus transformed into a prayer for the Spirit'' (p. 142).

13. See Chapter Three above.

14. Luke 24:43 means ''he ate at their table, or in their company or as their guest.'' The point is continuity, reunion and not the physical substance of the

risen body. This symbol invites us to look back at "those repeated meal scenes of the gospel in which Jesus was received as a guest and made his appeal to prospective followers in that capacity" (see Dillon, *Eye-Witnesses* 201).

15. A very helpful article on the grammar and significance of Luke 1:46–55, esp. 1:51–53, is: Jacques Dupont, "Le Magnificat comme discours sur Dieu," *NRT* 102 (1980) 321–43. See also the somewhat satisfactory abstract of Dupont's article: "The Magnificat as God-Talk," *TD* 29 (1981) 153–54. See further my article, "Mary's *Magnificat* and Recent Study," *Review for Religious* 42 (1983) 903–08.

16. See José P. Miranda, *Marx and the Bible: A Critique of the Philosophy of Oppression* (Maryknoll: Orbis, 1974) 217: "I wonder where there is more faith and hope: in believing 'in the God who raises the dead' (Rom. 4:17) or in believing like Luke in the God who 'filled the hungry with good things and sent the rich away empty' (Luke 1:53)?"

17. The Greek text is taken from *Psalmi cum Odis* (ed. Alfred Rahlfs; Septuaginta 10; 2d ed.; Goettingen: Vandenhoeck & Ruprecht, 1967). Note that Luke uses Psalm 22 in Luke 23:34 in his description of Jesus' death.

18. For more expansive comment, see Wimmer, *Fasting in the New Testament* 31–44, 47–51.

19. *Luke* 510.

20. See Chapter Three above for the nature of some of this opposition.

21. See Luke's description of the religious leaders in 14:7; 20:46 as those who seek places of honor at feasts. My use of the popular "being waited on hand and foot" is an attempt to convey some of the privileges the religious leaders expected as they reclined in the places of honor at festive banquets.

22. Note the threefold temptation which the crucified Jesus endures in Luke 23:35–39.

23. For a bibliography on Luke 6:20–49, see Fitzmyer, *Luke* 645–46.

24. "You shall be satisfied" seems to be a clear allusion to the Old Testament image of the "messianic banquet." See, e.g., Isa 25:6: "On this mountain the Lord of hosts will make for all peoples a feast of fat things, a feast of wine on the lees, of fat things full of marrow, of wine on the lees well refined."

25. An excellent article on how the theme of "hearing" runs throughout Luke 8:4–21 is: Jacques Dupont, "La parabole du semeur dans la version de Luc," in *Apophoreta: Festschrift fuer Ernst Haenchen zu seinem siebzigsten Geburtstag am 10. December 1964* (BZNW 30: Berlin: Toepelmann, 1964) 97–108.

26. See Marshall, *Luke* 324–25: "Implicitly, therefore, Luke identifies the sower with Jesus. . . ."

27. See Fitzmyer, *Luke* 707 on Luke 8:9–10: "human beings will be

charmed by the simplicity of the parable-preaching of Jesus and yet fail to understand what it should mean to them.''

28. *Birth of the Messiah* 316–19.

29. A representative bibliography on Mary as the model disciple in Luke is the following: Patrick J. Bearsley, "Mary the Perfect Disciple: A Paradigm for Mariology," *TS* 41 (1980) 461–504; *Mary in the New Testament* (ed. Raymond E. Brown et al; Philadelphia: Fortress; New York: Paulist, 1978) 105–77; Segundo Galilea, *Following Jesus* (Maryknoll: Orbis, 1981) 110–19.

30. Raymond E. Brown, "Mary in the New Testament and in Catholic Life," *America* 146, #19 (May 15, 1982) 379.

31. The attentive reader will recall that Jesus' "food temptation" occurred in the desert (4:1). Here, too, he is obedient to his Father's plan and feeds the hungry.

32. See again Isa 25:6 where God's promise of plenty is cast in the imagery of a banquet.

33. See the first beatitude of Luke 6:20: "Blessed are you poor, for yours is the kingdom of God.''

34. Later in this chapter—in the section on Jesus as a glutton and a drunkard—we will give further nuance to the reasons adduced here to answer the question of how Jesus got himself crucified.

35. Dillon, *Eye-Witnesses* 107; emphasis in original.

36. I follow Marshall, *Luke* 302, who views "a glutton and a drunkard" as a proverb. Fitzmyer, *Luke* 681 is of the opinion that this phrase does not echo Deut 21:20 in the Septuagint. While that may be true, Deut 21:18–21 is a helpful parallel for the meaning of the phrase. In a society which used the language of food and which separated the "in" group from the "out" group by means of food, it speaks volumes that Jesus was considered "a glutton and a drunkard.''

37. Tax collectors occur frequently in Luke's Gospel. See also 3:12; 5:27,29–30; 7:29; 18:9–14; 19:2. These are Jews involved in collecting indirect taxes (tolls, tariffs, imposts, customs) from various areas in Palestine for the Romans. They are associated with "sinners" because of the dishonesty which often characterized their activity. See Fitzmyer, *Luke* 469,592. The pejorative connotations of "tax collector" (*telōnēs*) would not be lost on Luke's non-Palestinian, non-Jewish readers. See Dio Chrysostom, *Oratio* 14.14 where he mentions collecting taxes and keeping a brothel as two occupations which, although not expressly forbidden by the laws, are considered base and unseemly by humankind. I am indebted to Ramsay MacMullen, *Roman Social Relations 50 B.C. to A.D. 284* (New Haven: Yale University, 1974) 140 for this reference to Dio Chrysostom. MacMullen's entire appendix on "The Lexicon of Snobbery" (pp. 138–41) would inform a cross-cultural reading of Luke-Acts.

38. See Marshall, *Luke* 302. Note also that the proverb of Deut 21 is literally true in Jesus' case: he eats and drinks.

39. See Norman Perrin, *Rediscovering the Teaching of Jesus* (New York: Harper & Row, 1967) 102–08. "Scribe, tax collector, fisherman and Zealot came together around the table at which they celebrated the joy of the present experience and anticipated its consummation in the future" (p. 107).

40. *New Testament Theology: The Proclamation of Jesus* (New York: Scribner's, 1971) 115–16.

41. *Luke* 302. Fitzmyer, *Luke* 677 is also of the opinion that the "you" of "you say" refers to the religious leaders. It should also be noted that the religious leaders are not "children of Wisdom" (7:35). Is not Luke subtly referring to the "righteous one" theme of Wis 2:10–20; 4:20–5:8? Jesus and John the Baptist are righteous followers of Wisdom. The religious leaders are not. I owe this insight to Jan Dijkman.

42. *Fasting in the New Testament* 112.

43. "The Ethic of Election in Luke's Great Banquet Parable," in *Essays in Old Testament Ethics (J. Philip Hyatt, In Memoriam)* (ed. James L. Crenshaw; John T. Willis; New York: Ktav, 1974) 247–71. See also Sanders' *God Has a Story Too: Sermons in Context* (Philadelphia: Fortress, 1979) 80–89.

44. See Sanders, "The Ethic of Election," 262.

45. *Private Morality in Greece and Rome: Some Historical Aspects* (Mnemosyne 57; Leiden: Brill, 1979) 132; see also p. 129. See further A.R. Hands, *Charities and Social Aid in Greece and Rome* (Ithaca: Cornell University Press, 1968) 138–39.

46. See X. de Meeus, "Composition de Lc. XIV, et genre symposiaque," *ETL* 37 (1961) 847–70.

47. See David E. Aune, "Septem Sapientium Convivium (Moralia 146B–164D)," in *Plutarch's Ethical Writings and Early Christian Literature* (ed. H.D. Betz; Studia ad Corpus Hellenisticum Novi Testamenti 4; Leiden: Brill, 1978) 51–105, esp. pp. 69–78.

48. The translation is taken from the Loeb Classical Library. Lucian's *Convivium* is also called *The Carousal* or *The Lapiths*.

49. See below, esp. on Luke 22:24–27.

50. The RSV text of Luke 14:1 has "to dine." The repetition of the Greek *phagein arton* (to eat bread) seems quite significant in a passage where Luke clearly distinguishes various kinds of feasting with different vocabulary: "to eat bread" (*phagein arton*) in 14:1,15; "to a marriage feast" (*eis gamous*) in 14:8; "give a dinner or a banquet" (*poiēs ariston ē deipnon*) in 14:12; "give a feast" (*dochēn poiēs*) in 14:13; "banquet" (*deipnon*) in 14:16,17,24.

51. Jesus' authority to heal on a sabbath seems to be the main issue behind

Luke 14:1–6. Yet its inclusion in the symposium of 14:1–24 shows that the question of who eats bread with whom is also at issue. There was no place for the man with dropsy at the festive meal of the religious leaders.

52. *The Jesus of the Parables* (Philadelphia: United Church Press, 1975) 126.

53. Sanders, "The Ethic of Election," emphasizes the double entendre behind the Greek word, *kaleō*, which is usually translated by "to invite" in Luke 14:1–24. It also means "to elect." "*Keklemenoi* ('those invited') in Luke means 'apparently elect' or 'those who consider themselves elected'" (p. 259).

54. It seems that Luke 14:24 is spoken by Jesus and not by the householder. Previously, the householder had been speaking to one servant; in 14:24 he is described as addressing more than one person, for "you" is plural. So Jesus is the one who invites. See Joachim Jeremias, *The Parables of Jesus* (New York: Scribner's, 1963) 177.

55. The invitation goes out to those outside the city gates, to the tramps and homeless, who live along the country roads and vineyard hedges. See Jeremias, *Parables* 64, 177.

56. See ibid., 177: "even the poorest, with oriental courtesy, modestly resist the invitation to the entertainment until they are taken by the hand and gently forced to enter the house."

57. On all of Luke 14:1–24, see now the unpublished M.A. thesis of Anne Marie Sweet, "Luke 14:1–24: A Synthesis of Luke's Theology of the Shared Meal" (Chicago: Catholic Theological Union, 1983).

58. On Luke 22:14–38 as a farewell discourse, see Eugene A. LaVerdiere, "A Discourse at the Last Supper," *The Bible Today* 72 (March, 1974) 1540–48.

59. A translation of the Testament of Joseph may be found in *The Apocrypha and Pseudepigrapha of the Old Testament in English* (ed. R.H. Charles; Oxford: Clarendon, 1913), 2.346–54.

60. On the ethical force of the patriarch's last words, see Walter Harrelson, "The Significance of 'Last Words' for Intertestamental Ethics," in *Essays in Old Testament Ethics* 203–13, esp. p. 210: "The prototypes of envy, hatred, or jealousy are men of Israel's past, on whom the life of God's people has depended. Despite their failings, they were used by God to fulfil his purposes. And more—though they were given opportunity to repent and mend their ways, and did so, the stories clearly indicate that their change of heart did not come about easily. Their repentance was no easy thing, and they were recipients of no cheap grace."

61. The reader might also want to check other, earlier Lukan indications of the passion and resurrection: 2:31–35; 2:41–52; 4:16–30.

62. Luke 22:19b–20 is original. See E. Earle Ellis, *The Gospel of Luke*

(New Century Bible; 2d ed.; London: Oliphants, 1974) 236: "The longer text in all probability is what the Evangelist wrote." I do not have the space here to argue against those who contend that Luke places little, if any, soteriological value on Jesus' death on the cross. See Chapter Five below. It must be remembered that Luke is not Paul and that Luke is a kerygmatic story teller and not a dogmatician. Fitzmyer, *Luke* 221 is to be congratulated for a splendid observation which must be developed: "Finally, one should recall what was said above (p. 23) about the episode of Jesus and the penitent thief, which is a Lucan symbolic way of highlighting the effect of the crucified Jesus on human beings." Contrast Brian E. Beck, "'*Imitatio Christi*,'" 37: "The evidence suggests that we should assign 22:19f to one of the other elements in Luke's total picture rather than to the martyr theme, and, in view of his overall treatment of the death of Jesus, perhaps regard this passage, along with the less precise Acts 20:28, as unassimilated fragments of pre-Lucan tradition, or at least subsidiary strands in his thought, rather than conscious formulations intended to be regulative of the whole narrative." Again, Luke is judged by the canons of Western, non-narrative logic and found wanting.

63. "Luke's Sacramental Theology," 326.

64. Arthur Vööbus is exceptionally fine on Luke's exhortatory intent in Luke 22:14–38. See his *The Prelude to the Lukan Passion Narrative* 11–54. On p. 39 Vööbus writes: "The ultimate motivation in the composition of the evangelist is that of actualization and confrontation. . . . Instead of the past event, that which is brought to the fore is the present reality of Christ and His present relationship to the believers. The once for all character of the event receives an entirely different complexion—it is actualized and its immediate character is made vital for the contemporary congregation and its life." See now Dennis M. Sweetland, "The Lord's Supper and the Lukan Community," *BTB* 13 (1983) 23–27.

65. See Robert Tannehill, "A Study in the Theology of Luke-Acts," *ATR* 43 (1961) 195–203, esp. p. 203: "In the conferral of the kingdom on the apostles we see that the church participates in the kingdom through Jesus' death. Luke rarely speaks of the death of Jesus in the manner in which we might expect, especially when we come to him from reading Paul, but in his own way he makes clear that that death was a death 'for us.'"

66. See Joachim Jeremias, *The Eucharistic Words of Jesus* (New York: Scribner's, 1966) 254–55 for a differently worded, but similar interpretation of "in memory of me": that God may remember Jesus and his kingly work and complete it.

67. See S. Brown, *Apostasy and Perseverance* 9.

68. The disciples do not abandon Jesus and will be present at the cross (see 23:49, "all his acquaintances," and the discussion of that phrase in Chapter Five

below), but they will need to have their eyes opened by the risen Jesus to see, in faith, the full meaning of Jesus' journey of effecting God's justice.

69. On the meaning of Luke 22:36, see Martin Hengel, *Was Jesus a Revolutionist?* (Facet Books, Biblical Series 28; Philadelphia: Fortress, 1971) 23: "In no case can one see in it (Luke 22:36) a demand for armed revolt." See also H. Merkel, "Zealot," *IDBSup* 981: "It (Luke 22:36b) can be understood as a paradoxically formulated allusion to the temptations and persecutions which the disciples will encounter."

70. "Luke's Sacramental Theology," 326–30.

Chapter Five

LUKE 23 AND LUKE'S THEMATIC CHRISTOLOGY AND SOTERIOLOGY

In Chapters Two, Three, and Four we dealt with the question of how Jesus got himself crucified. Or put another way, we explored the antecedents of Luke 23, Luke's passion account. As God's righteous one who revealed God's way of justice and as the prophetic embodiment of God's good news to the poor, Jesus challenged accepted views of justice and fed a hungry creation as he shared food with the unjust and outcasts. He ran foul of the arrogant, unjust, self-seeking, self-righteous ones, symbolized by the religious leaders, who plotted his death in Jerusalem, the city of promise and fulfillment, the city which kills the prophets (Luke 13:33–34). Now in this chapter we come to Jesus' crucifixion, to the critical point in Luke's narrative of Jesus' journey of revealing who God is, a faithful God who wills to be with his creation in and through death.

In this chapter our goal is twofold. Through a study of the themes of Luke 23 we will attain our first goal: to offer a new reading of Luke's passion account, for all of us readers know the passion account so well in a harmonized version that we do not come to Luke 23 with fresh minds, hearts, and imaginations. As van Unnik sagely comments:

> the Lukan passion account is very dramatic. For people who read it for the first time—alas, we know it too well in advance!—the story unfolds like a tragedy. The confession of the criminal crucified with Jesus and Jesus' last word, 'Father, into your hands I commend my spirit' (23:46) partially reveal

the identity of the main character of the drama. The drama does not concern some tragic hero, but the very Son of God.[1]

Secondly, our thematic study of Luke 23 will illumine Luke's view of the God of Jesus and how he saves. Through the pursuit of the Lukan thematics, all of which come to a fullness of expression in this climactic chapter, we will be able to give some explanation for the fact that Luke does not view Jesus' death as an expiation for sin.[2] In Luke-Acts Jesus' death is not an isolated event, but is a part of Jesus' entire life of revealing a faithful God. The theme of food, explored in Chapter Four and to be pursued again in this chapter, reveals a God who wants to sit down at table with all men and women and will remove all obstacles, even that of death, which stand in the way of the accomplishment of that communion. The theme of justice, probed earlier in Chapter Three and to be treated again in this chapter, makes manifest what the Lukan soteriological question is: Is God or evil in charge of God's creation and people? That is, it is a question of God's fidelity to the promises of life he has given with creation and election. Can God deliver on his promises? So far in the Lukan narrative of Jesus, God's righteous one, that question has been written and answered not in spatial or temporal images, but with personal imagery and in human form. In the events of Luke 23 God reveals his will to be with Jesus and thus with his creation, even in the darkest moments of injustice and crucifixion of the innocent. And as is to be expected from Luke's narrative so far, there will be diverse responses to that revelation. And many of the personal responses to that revelation will be imaged by ''seeing''—the symbol for accepting revelation.

We will accomplish our two goals in this way. After providing the orientation of a sentence-outline of the sequence of events in Luke 23, we will delve into the Lukan themes found in this sequence of events. We will concentrate primarily on the themes of the faithful God, justice, and food and will examine in passing other Lukan themes such as Jerusalem, way, witness, divine necessity, mercy, conversion, seeing, women, universalism, clothing, and today.[3]

Because of the thematic approach developed in this chapter, it will not be possible to supply a detailed exegesis of every verse of Luke 23.[4] Also it is not possible to deal with questions of historicity.[5] Nor is it possible to examine the question of the literary genre of Luke 23.[6] Moreover, it is not possible to deal with the rich thematic similarities between Luke 23 and John 18–19.[7] Our thematic approach does not allow us the opportunity to discuss the question of Luke's possible political intent.[8] Finally, we must forego a discussion of the sources of Luke's passion account.[9]

SENTENCE-OUTLINE OF SEQUENCE OF EVENTS IN LUKE 23

Luke 23:1–5	All the religious leaders accuse Jesus before Pilate of leading the people astray and of being a king.
Luke 23:6–12	Jesus is silent before Herod, who had wanted to see him.
Luke 23:13–25	Pilate releases the guilty Barabbas and hands the guiltless Jesus over to the will of the religious leaders and the people.
Luke 23:26	Simon of Cyrene carries Jesus' cross behind him.
Luke 23:27–34a	Jesus, the rejected prophet, warns the daughters of Jerusalem to repent and offers forgiveness to God's enemies.
Luke 23:34b–39	The people, who are watching, are contrasted with the religious leaders. The religious leaders, the soldiers, and one crucified evil doer tempt Jesus, the savior.
Luke 23:40–43	Jesus, the prophet, promises that the repentant evil-doer, who had tried to convert his fellow, will eat with him in paradise.
Luke 23:44–45	Heaven and earth respond to Jesus' death, which opens a new way to God.
Luke 23:46	Jesus, the obedient and suffering righteous one, confidently places himself in his Father's care.
Luke 23:47–49	Those who see know the true meaning of Jesus' death and respond accordingly: a pagan, the crowd, Jesus' acquaintances, and women disciples from Galilee.
Luke 23:50–56	Joseph of Arimathea, a righteous person, the one religious leader who did not consent to Jesus'

death, gives up one of his cherished possessions,
his tomb, for Jesus. The women disciples see how
Jesus is buried.

In depicting this sequence of events, I have almost set them down in
chronicle form: Jesus on trial, Jesus on his way to the cross, Jesus crucified, Jesus' death and burial. Yet as is obvious, there is much more
meaning to these events than a chronicle-like sequence might lead us to
believe. Our probing of the Lukan themes will set us upon the path of
finding that deeper meaning.

LUKE 23:1–5

¹Then the whole company of them arose, and brought him before Pilate. ²And they began to accuse him, saying, 'We found
this man perverting our nation, and forbidding us to give trib-
ute to Caesar, and saying that he himself is Christ a king.'
³And Pilate asked him, 'Are you the King of the Jews?' And
he answered him, 'You have said so.' ⁴And Pilate said to the
chief priests and the multitudes, 'I find no crime in this man.'
⁵But they were urgent, saying, 'He stirs up the people, teaching throughout all Judea, from Galilee even to this place.'

From its opening chapters the Lukan kerygmatic narrative has been
moving toward this point—Jesus on trial. And lest we miss the import of
Luke's version of Jesus' trial and crucifixion, it is vitally important for
us, at the very beginning of our discussion of Luke 23, to remind ourselves of what has led Jesus to this rendezvous in Jerusalem. Our memory lesson will also provide us the opportunity of acquainting ourselves
with the themes of Luke 23:1–5.

Jesus

A glance back over the contents of Chapter One would show that
the Jesus on trial in Jerusalem is the righteous one who has been faithful
to God's will and kingdom. Not only is Jesus, the individual, on trial,

but also his integrity and his God are on trial. Will God rescue his righteous one, his Son, from the hands of his persecutors?

That same Chapter One informed us readers about the Lukan motif of "rejected prophet." Jesus, an individual, is not the only one being rejected. God's message, God himself, is being rejected. The religious leaders have stopped their ears from hearing the message of God's good news to the poor and outcast. In Jerusalem, which rejects the prophets, they bring Jesus to trial.

Earlier in the Gospel Luke had described Jesus as the agent of God's kingdom. Beginning in 19:38 and continuing through this chapter (see 23:2,3,37–38,42,51), Luke stresses that Jesus is a king.[10] Thus at the end of Luke's narrative it has become quite clear about what kind of king the angel Gabriel was speaking in 1:32–33. Jesus, as king, exercises God's rule of giving release to captives (23:12–25) and of giving the bread of life to outcasts (23:39–43). Jesus is the embodiment of God's kingdom.

Pilate and others in Chapter 23 will repeatedly declare that Jesus is innocent. See 23:4,14,15,22,41,47,51. Jesus, the suffering righteous one and the rejected prophet, is also the martyr, who despite persecution and rejection is faithful to the mission which his God has entrusted to him. He is a man of integrity, whose death is part of God's plan (Luke 9:23; 13:33; 17:25; 22:37,42; 24:7,26,46). And Jesus obediently carries out his God's plan (Luke 9:51; 13:33; 17:25; 22:37,42). He goes freely, unbound, to his trial and to his death, confident of his God's power to save his innocently suffering righteous ones from ultimate defeat and separation.

The Religious Leaders

As we have seen time after time in previous chapters, especially Chapter Three, the religious leaders are stereotypes of those folks who oppose a justice life-style. They are stereotypes of human perversity. They are in league with the power of darkness (see 22:53). In 23:1–5 they are true to their typecasting as they pervert the meaning of what Jesus has said about money and Caesar (20:20–26). In their eyes Jesus has been perverting the people by imaging an alien God through his table fellowship with sinners and outcasts. Jesus, "a glutton and a drunkard" (7:34), must die for the way he has eaten.

But in using the religious leaders as stereotypes of humanity's un-just attacks against the innocent, Luke does not paint a thoroughgoing bleak picture of the human condition. Note how at the end of Luke 23 he describes Joseph of Arimathea: "He was a member of the council, a good and righteous man, who had not consented to their purpose and deed, and he was looking for the kingdom of God" (23:50–51). This de-scription is at odds with 22:70 and 23:1, which stress that *all* members of the council were in consort against Jesus. Human sinfulness is never so pervasive that God's word of life and kingly rule of justice cannot find receptive minds and hearts.

In summary, although Luke 22:69 anticipatorily trumpets God's victory for Jesus, the Son of Man, over the power of darkness, 23:1–5 gives little hint of that victory. Wisdom 2:17–18 is an excellent sum-mary of the dynamics of 23:1–5: "Let us see if his words are true, and let us test what will happen at the end of his life; for if the righteous man is God's son, he will help him, and will deliver him from the hand of his adversaries."

LUKE 23:6 –12

⁶When Pilate heard this, he asked whether the man was a Gal-ilean. ⁷And when he learned that he belonged to Herod's juris-diction, he sent him over to Herod, who was himself in Jerusalem at that time. ⁸When Herod saw Jesus, he was very glad, for he had long desired to see him, because he had heard about him, and he was hoping to see some sign done by him. ⁹So he questioned him at some length; but he made no answer. ¹⁰The chief priests and the scribes stood by, vehemently ac-cusing him. ¹¹And Herod with his soldiers treated him with contempt and mocked him; then, arraying him in gorgeous (white) apparel, he sent him back to Pilate. ¹²And Herod and Pilate became friends with each other that very day, for before this they had been at enmity with each other.

Most of the secondary literature which deals with this passage is taken up with the question, "Why did Pilate hand Jesus over to Herod Anti-pas?"[11] But there is enough secondary literature on the themes of this passage to build a case that this apparent literary detour also fits into Luke's recapitulation of themes in Luke 23.

Reconciliation

In this thematic interpretation of 23:6–12, the accent falls on the last verse: "And Herod and Pilate became friends with each other that very day, for before this they had been at enmity with each other." On the very day—today—that Jesus dies, the effects of his death are felt in history. Two bitter enemies forgive one another.[12] This motif of reconciliation is found in other places in Luke's Gospel, often finding expression as forgiveness or peace.[13] It is also found in 23:34a in Jesus' prayer for his Father's forgiveness of his enemies. In his justice God does forgive the debt of sin through Jesus' death and reconciles Jew and Gentile to himself.

Suffering Righteous One

Luke says explicitly in 23:9 that Jesus was silent. And although Luke does not say so explicitly in 23:13–25, Jesus is silent during that scene too. Time after time we have seen that Luke's Gospel portrays Jesus as the righteous one. Building upon one of the most powerful literary and theological models of the suffering righteous one—the Suffering Servant of Yahweh—Luke alludes to Isaiah 53:7 in 23:9. In the New American Bible translation of Isaiah 53:7 we read: "Though he was harshly treated, he submitted and opened not his mouth; like a lamb led to the slaughter or a sheep before the shearers, he was silent and opened not his mouth." As the obedient and loving doer of his Father's will, Jesus, the righteous one, is treated unjustly. And as we will see in more detail during our consideration of 23:13–25, Jesus' silence is not that of despair, but that of utmost trust in his Father God.

Clothing—Gorgeous [White] Apparel

Space limitations do not allow us to enter deeply into Luke's thematic of clothing. Some general indications will have to suffice. Luke begins his Gospel with two references to the babe Jesus in swaddling clothes (2:7,11). As Raymond E. Brown says so well: "His swaddling does not belie his royal role."[14] Skipping over many other references to clothing, we come to 19:36: "And as he rode along, they spread their garments on the road." This passage occurs in a context wherein Jesus is hailed as king (19:38). As I. Howard Marshall aptly comments on 19:36: "The placing of garments for the animal to walk over is another expression of respect, perhaps indicating willingness to let a ruler trample on one's own property. . . ."[15] In 23:11 Jesus is robed in "gorgeous [white] apparel." In 23:34 he is stripped naked. In 23:53 he is clothed in linen. In 24:12 the risen Jesus leaves the linen behind in the tomb.

In a sense Luke describes Jesus' life from beginning to end by means of the theme of clothing. Perhaps we will arrive at a better understanding of the "gorgeous [white] apparel" of 23:11 by looking at the other references to clothing in the immediate context, i.e., 23:34,53; 24:12. In 23:34b Jesus, the prisoner, about to die by crucifixion, is stripped of his clothes. As Edgar Haulotte observes, in biblical culture to be deprived of clothing was to lose one's identity.[16] Haulotte goes on to say that persons whose liberty had been definitively taken away lose the capacity to wear clothing. Such people are prisoners and slaves (see Deut 28:48 and Isa 20:2–4), prostitutes (Ez 16:38–40), mad/demented people (1 Sam 19:23–24), and damned folks (see 1 Sam 28:14). These people have no control over their lives.[17] From having the gorgeous white apparel covering his nakedness, Jesus is reduced to utter humiliation. Symbolically, he has lost his identity.

The meaning of the linen clothing of 23:53 and 24:12 is difficult for us modern wearers of synthetic clothing to appreciate. As Johannes Quasten has pointed out, linen at the time of Luke was a symbol of immortality.[18] It came from flax, which came from the earth, which was immortal. It was contrasted with wool which came from animals, which perish. As a symbol of faith in God's power to resurrect the just, Jesus is clothed in linen in 23:53. But as a symbol that he enjoys the reality symbolized by the linen, the risen Jesus leaves the linen behind in the place of death in 24:12.

With the above background on Luke's theme of clothing in mind, let us return to 23:11. Paul Joüon is probably correct that the "gorgeous apparel" is a white mantle.[19] I have followed his interpretation by adding "white" in brackets to the RSV's translation of 23:11. It is probable that "gorgeous apparel" does not refer to royal/kingly clothing. Luke uses "gorgeous apparel" only one other time in his writings (Acts 10:30) to refer to the man who appears to Cornelius with an extraordinary message. And when Luke wants to refer to royal/kingly clothing, he has the vocabulary with which to do that, as in Acts 12:21. With the exception of 13:31–33, every time that Luke introduces Herod he specifically mentions that he is a tetrarch, not a king.[20] A tetrarch does not own the kingly garments with which to doll up the innocent Jesus.

If the gorgeous apparel which Jesus wears does not portray him as a king, then what is its meaning? A clue is found in Polybius, *The Histories* X 4.9–5.1 where the "gorgeous apparel" (*lampran esthēta*) means the white garment (*toga candida*) which a candidate for office wore.[21] The candidate would appear in the forum and would be selected by the populace for office. Herod decks the innocent Jesus out in a white mantle and thus prepares him for the selection of the religious leaders and the people in 23:13–25. The irony of the next scene, 23:13–25, is that the people and the religious leaders select Barabbas and not the innocent Jesus, clad in his white gorgeous apparel. And with further irony the rejected king Jesus will be depicted as stripped of his candidate clothes and identity in 23:34 only to exercise the vast kingly powers of granting life—today—to the repentant evil-doer (23:42–43).

Seeing

The final theme to occupy our attention in Luke 23:6–12 is seeing. It occurs thrice in 23:8: "When Herod saw Jesus, he was very glad, for he had long desired to see him, because he had heard about him, and he was hoping to see some sign done by him." Perhaps the best single text to use as a sample of the theme of seeing is found in Acts 26:17–18 where Paul talks about his commission from the Lord Jesus: "delivering you from the people and from the Gentiles—to whom I send you to open their eyes, that they may turn from darkness to light and from the power of Satan to God, that they may receive forgiveness of sins and a place among those who are sanctified by faith in me."[22] To see is to see deeply, to see with the eyes of faith, to be converted and to walk in the light. Herod is not able to see who Jesus is. He wants a miracle from Jesus, but receives none.

Within the immediate context of 23:8 "seeing" occurs a number of times in significant ways. After asking for Jesus' crucifixion, the people are narrated as "watching" in 23:35 and are contrasted with the religious leaders who scoff at Jesus. While it is dark, the centurion sees (23:47), the multitudes see (23:48), and all his acquaintances and the women disciples see. Furthermore, there is a great thematic to-do about seeing in Luke 24. See 24:12,16,24,31,32,39,45.[23] What have they seen? What has the centurion seen that he says of Jesus, "Certainly this man was innocent/righteous"? What did the crowds/people see that caused them to beat their breasts in repentance? For our present purposes I suggest that they have seen God's revelation in Jesus. That is, their sight is not just physical sight, but the sight which is response to revelation.

As we move through the rest of Luke 23, I would propose the following pattern as a means of ascertaining Luke's meaning:

23:8 and 23:47	Contrast the two "seeings": Herod wants to see a miracle and cannot; the pagan centurion does see the miracle of Jesus' death.
23:35 and 23:48	Note what the people/crowds see which prompts them to repent.
23:49 and Luke 24	Note what the eleven, the women, and the rest do see.

In summary, in this section we have again made contact with the Lukan themes of innocently suffering righteous one and God's justice. At the same time our appreciation of Luke's view of christology and soteriology has been enriched by sampling his themes of clothing and seeing. It will not surprise us to find that many of these same themes recur in our next section, 23:13–25.

LUKE 23:13–25

[13]Pilate then called together the chief priests and the rulers and the people, [14]and said to them, 'You brought me this man as one who was perverting the people; and after examining him before you, behold, I did not find this man guilty of any of your charges against him; [15]neither did Herod, for he sent him

back to us. Behold, nothing deserving death has been done by him; [16]I will therefore chastise him and release him.' [18]But they all cried out together, 'Away with this man, and release to us Barabbas'—[19]a man who had been thrown into prison for an insurrection started in the city, and for murder. [20]Pilate addressed them once more, desiring to release Jesus; [21]but they shouted out, 'Crucify, crucify him!' [22]A third time he said to them, 'Why, what evil has he done? I have found in him no crime deserving death; I will therefore chastise him and release him.' [23]But they were urgent, demanding with loud cries that he should be crucified. And their voices prevailed. [24]So Pilate gave sentence that their demand should be granted. [25]He released the man who had been thrown into prison for insurrection and murder, whom they asked for; but Jesus he delivered up to their will.

Dramatic Structure of Luke 23:13–25

The well-balanced structure of 23:13–25 helps carry the themes found in this passage: the rejection of the innocently suffering righteous one and king; Jesus' death will release those held prisoners; the involvement of "the people" (ho laos) in the rejection of Jesus.

(1) 23:13	Pilate is together with all Israel—leaders and people.
(2) 23:14–15	Pilate declares Jesus innocent twice.
(3) 23:16	Pilate wants to release Jesus after chastisement.
(a) 23:18	Nation replies, "Take him away. Release Barabbas."
23:19 gives a description of Barabbas	
(4) 23:20	Pilate wants to release Jesus.
(a) 23:21	Nation responds, "Crucify, crucify him!"
(5) 23:22	Pilate finds Jesus innocent for the third time and for the third time he wants to release Jesus, after chastisement.

(a) 23:23   Nation demands that Jesus be crucified.
(6) 23:24–25   Pilate releases Barabbas, who is described
                    again as in 23:19, and gives Jesus over to their
                    will.

This structural analysis of 23:13–25 clearly indicates how the nation is vying with Pilate over the two candidates, Jesus and Barabbas. Although Jesus is the superior candidate because of his innocence, attested three times, he is rejected three times by the nation in favor of a convicted malefactor. Luke's drama of Jesus' passion is at a peak here. And as we will see below in our study of the themes present in this passage, Luke's dramatic artistry is at the service of his theology.

Jesus Is the Innocently Suffering Righteous One

Robed still in his gorgeous white apparel as a candidate for the office of king, Jesus is pitted over against Barabbas, whom Luke twice describes as an insurrectionist and as a murderer. Pilate, who has the power of life and death in his judicial hands, thrice declares that Jesus is innocent and thrice tries to release Jesus. But the power of darkness prevails, and the innocent one is condemned to crucifixion.

With his story-telling artistry Luke uses 23:13–25 as a means of showing how Jesus saves. Jesus dies to save a person imprisoned for crimes deserving crucifixion. And in doing so, Jesus fulfills God's promise as revealed earlier in the Gospel during his inaugural sermon in his hometown synagogue at Nazareth (4:16–30). By his crucifixion Jesus not only proclaims release to those imprisoned, but actually frees them from their bonds. From 4:16–30 to this passage Luke has not narrated an instance in which Jesus frees a prisoner. Now at the climactic point in his narrative he portrays Jesus, at the lowest point of his powers, as the liberator of prisoners.

And amazing as it is that the apparently powerless Jesus grants freedom from imprisonment to an outcast of society, it is even more amazing that he does this through his silence. As we mentioned in our treatment of 23:6–12, the allusion here is to the silence of the innocently suffering righteous servant of Isaiah 53:7. Jesus' silence is not that of despair, or of lack of resolution, or of indifference to injustice. It is the silence of trust. It is the silence which reveals his intimacy with his Father God. This silence is powerful in its effects of liberation. And the attentive reader should note that when Jesus does speak in 23:28–31,34,43,46, he speaks out of the depths of his relationship with his Father God. He, who trustingly places his life in the hands of his Father God, forgives and offers the bread of life to others, thus delivering them from the hands of the power of darkness.

The People as Those Who Are Generally Open to God's Kingly Rule

In Chapter Three above, during our discussion of Luke 7:29–30, we broached the subject of "the people" in relationship to the religious leaders. We noted that Luke equates people with multitudes/crowds. We also pointed out that whereas the religious leaders are generally stereotypes of an unjust life-style, the people are representatives of those who are generally open to God's kingly rule as embodied in Jesus. There is no need to rehearse the various passages, especially within the Jerusalem phase of Jesus' ministry, which support my observations.

What is important to note in 23:13–25, especially in 23:13,18,21, is that people are intimately involved in the demand that Jesus be crucified. Those who are representatives of folks who are generally open to God's kingly rule are described as closed. They, too, ask for the death of the righteous one and prophet of God's good news to the poor. It seems that the power of darkness has vanquished all humanity. Yet the passion narrative is not finished with 23:13–25. Luke will have more to say about the people/multitude/crowds in 23:27,35,48. They are not so stiff-necked that they cannot repent of their rejection of Jesus. Luke's narrative will describe them following Jesus and will describe their repentance in 23:35 and 23:48 with the symbol of "seeing." The people/crowd repent once their eyes are opened by faith to see what God effects through the death of Jesus, the righteous one, e.g., the paradisiacal life for the repentant malefactor (23:40–43).

In sum, our exploration of Luke 23:13–25 has shown us some more aspects of the Lukan theme of the innocently suffering righteous one. We have renewed acquaintances with the theme of the people. And in passing, we noted the theme of liberation from imprisonment and the theme of repentance. And it is of paramount importance to remember that it is not just Jesus who is on trial in Luke's passion account, but it is also and especially the faithful God of Jesus and of all righteous ones who is on trial. Is that God true to his promises of life for his creatures?

LUKE 23:26

[26]And as they led him away, they seized one Simon of Cyrene, who was coming in from the country, and laid on him the cross, to carry it behind Jesus.

It seems the almost universal opinion of commentators that Simon of Cyrene is a model of discipleship. These authors refer to the similarity in wording between Luke 23:26 and Luke 9:23, 14:27, two discipleship passages which emphasize carrying one's cross behind Jesus.

What is not often noted, however, is that cross-bearing following of Jesus is contrasted here with the "following" of the great multitude of the people including women in 23:27. Simon has responded fully to his call to follow Jesus by bearing Jesus' cross whereas the people, who earlier called out for Jesus' crucifixion (23:13–25), follow without commitment. But as they follow Jesus to the cross, they will be warned by Jesus to repent (23:27–31). They will look upon the deep meaning of Jesus' death (23:35) and will end up beating their breasts in an initial wave of repentance (23:48).

It is also not frequently noted that Luke uses a special verb in 23:26, which is usually and inadequately translated as "they seized."[24] I would modify the RSV translation and render 23:26 thus: "And as they led him away, they laid friendly hands on one Simon of Cyrene, who was coming in from the country, and laid on him the cross, to carry it behind Jesus." To carry Jesus' cross is positive and an invitation to discipleship. This invitation can come quite unexpectedly as in Simon's case and as Luke's "daily" in 9:23 also indicates, for daily life is shot through with the unexpected. And it goes without saying that in Luke's Gospel to carry Jesus' cross is to be involved in his justice life-style and in preaching God's good news to the poor.

Simon shows that the way to salvation is to follow Jesus, who leads humanity in its journey to the faithful God.

LUKE 23:27–34[a]

[27]And there followed him a great multitude of the people, and of women who bewailed and lamented him. [28]But Jesus turning to them said, 'Daughters of Jerusalem, do not weep for me, but weep for yourselves and for your children. [29]For behold, the days are coming when they will say, "Blessed are the barren, and the wombs that never bore, and the breasts that never gave suck!" [30]Then they will begin to say to the mountains, "Fall on us"; and to the hills, "Cover us." [31]For if they do this when the wood is green, what will happen when it is dry?' [32]Two others also, who were criminals, were led away to be put to death with him. [33]And when they came to the place which is called The Skull, there they crucified him, and the criminals, one on the right and one on the left. [34]And Jesus said, 'Father, forgive them; for they know not what they do.'

This difficult passage deals with two major and very familiar Lukan themes, that of rejected prophet and that of innocently suffering righteous one. It also deals with the themes of repentance and people.

Jesus as the Rejected Prophet

As we saw in Chapter One above, one of the main features of the theme of rejected prophet is God's continual offer of forgiveness to those who reject his mercy. Because of this emphasis I have thought it best to include 23:32–34a in our discussion of the scene of the weeping daughters of Jerusalem. The prophet Jesus' call to repentance in 23:27–31 should not be isolated from God's offer of forgiveness in 23:32–34a, especially in 23:34a.[25] And in praying for forgiveness of his adversaries, Jesus is living out his own teaching as found in 6:27–28 and 17:4.

With this general thematic background in mind, we may be able to shed some clarity on some of the obscurities of 23:27–31. It seems abundantly clear that in 23:27–31 Luke is emphasizing repentance. The sovereign Jesus, who is prophet, and who doesn't need repentance because of his trust-filled union with his Father God, demands repentance of the people/multitudes/crowd which has just rejected him. Luke contrasts them with Simon of Cyrene (23:26), who follows Jesus by bearing his cross. The people merely follow Jesus, but even that is progress on the road to repentance, for earlier in the narrative (23:13–25) they had rejected the prophet Jesus.

Yet 23:31 is a troublesome verse and seems to go contrary to the repentance motif which rings so clearly throughout the rest of the passage. But in trying to answer such simple questions as "to what does green wood/tree refer?" and "to what does dry wood/tree refer?" we will discover that 23:31 also deals with the motif of repentance.

In discussing 23:31, I use the King James Version: "For if they do these things in a green tree, what shall be done in the dry?" This translation has the advantage of making the allusion to Ezekiel 17:24 more transparent. Ezekiel 17:24 in the NAB reads: "And all the trees of the field shall know that I, the Lord, bring low the high tree, lift high the lowly tree, wither up the green tree, and make the withered tree bloom. As I, the Lord, have spoken, so will I do."[26] If one accepts the tree imagery of Ezekiel 17:24 as the background for withered/dry tree, then "these things" refers to the rejection of Jesus who gives life as does a living, green tree.[27] And if human persons—note the "they" as subject—reject the green tree which gives life, what will happen to a dead or withered tree? This question is given two answers from the context. One is that the tree that does not give life will be destroyed, for failure to repent does have dire consequences (23:29–30). The other answer is that God continues to offer life to the dead—note the circumlocution for God's activity in the "what will happen" of 23:31. As the prophecy of Ezekiel 17:24 says, it is of God's nature to make the withered tree bloom, but to wither that tree which exalts itself in its security. And as Jesus, the prophet, prays in 23:34a, God can bring to life the withered tree of those who are repentant.

In sum, the major thrust of 23:27–31 seems to be Jesus' prophetic warning that the people repent. Human complicity in the rejection of God's prophet and kingdom does not shut the door to God's offer of forgiveness (see 23:34a). As their following of Jesus (23:27) and as their contemplation of Jesus' final hours (23:35) indicate, these folks are still open to God's prophetic message as embodied in Jesus. And they will be moved to conversion by what they see through the eyes of faith (23:48).

Jesus as the Innocently Suffering Righteous One

In 23:27–34a the theme of Jesus, the righteous one, is almost as strong as the theme of Jesus, the rejected prophet. Luke 23:32, "two others also, who were criminals, were led away to be put to death with him," refers back to Jesus' words in 22:37, "For I tell you that this scripture must be fulfilled in me, 'And he was reckoned with transgressors'; for what is written about me has its fulfillment." And these two verses are references to the innocently suffering righteous servant of Isaiah 53:12. As God's righteous one, Jesus obediently and lovingly goes along the path laid out for him by God. He wills to be with the outcasts of society during their darkest hours and thus embodies a God whose greatest longing is to be with his beleaguered creatures.

That Jesus, the persecuted righteous one, prays for his enemies (23:34a) speaks volumes about himself and about the God he preaches. This God will indeed vindicate his righteous ones, a theme which has pulsed through Luke's Gospel ever since Mary's Magnificat (1:46–55). But he will not vindicate them by destroying their oppressors. God's righteousness is manifested in his forgiveness of the oppressors of his righteous ones.[28] The God who rectifies a world gone astray from justice is the God who extends bounteous forgiveness and mercy, even to the unjust.

The Jesus who has been silent for so much of the Lukan passion account speaks the words of God in 23:27–34a. He trusts so deeply in God and is in such union with his Father God that his concern is not on himself, but upon those who lament his fate. In effect, he says that God will protect him and that the multitude should look to its own relationship with God. The Jesus whom Luke has described throughout his Gospel as a person of prayerful union with God prays at this decisive moment of his life. And he prays for others.[29] Obviously, Luke does not use the terminology of Nicea and Chalcedon in his presentation of Jesus and of his Father God. But the christology implied in 23:28–31,34a,43,46 is high indeed.

In summary, our analysis of 23:27–34a has contributed additional building blocks to our construction of Luke's christology and soteriology. And it is no coincidence that these building blocks are shot through with the colors of the themes of God's rejected prophet and righteous one.

LUKE 23:34^b–39

³⁴ᵇAnd they cast lots to divide his garments. ³⁵And the people stood by, watching; but the rulers scoffed at him, saying, 'He saved others; let him save himself, if he is the Christ of God, his Chosen One!' ³⁶The soldiers also mocked him, coming up and offering him vinegar, ³⁷and saying, 'If you are the King of the Jews, save yourself!' ³⁸There was also an inscription over him, 'This is the King of the Jews.' ³⁹One of the criminals who were hanged railed at him, saying, 'Are you not the Christ? Save yourself and us!'

For all its brevity this is one of the richest passages in Luke 23. A brief tour of its themes will disclose some of its wealth.

Structure

Even a cursory glance at the parallel accounts of this scene in Mark, Matthew, and John would show to what extent Luke's account is streamlined. He has achieved a certain dramatic effect by streamlining the sequence of revilers. There are three groups of revilers, and each is clearly separated from the other. And Albert Vanhoye may well be correct when he observes:

> The taunts are grouped according to a different order, which brings about a new perspective. One can note at the outset that there is a descending order in the dignity of the persons concerned. . . . There comes last of all the turn of the two malefactors. That Jesus is scorned even by his companions in torment is indeed the climax of humiliation.³⁰

Jesus as the Innocently Suffering Righteous One

This theme is so deeply inbedded in the familiar Lukan and gospel narrative that we may easily miss it. Within 23:34b–39 and also in 23:46 and perhaps even in 23:49, there is reference to the innocently suffering righteous one. This reference is made via allusion to the Book of Wisdom and to the Old Testament psalms of the innocently suffering righteous one, who trusts courageously and profoundly in God for salvation. In what follows I will first give translations of the relevant Old Testament materials and pair them with the Lukan texts.[31] Then I will explain the significance of these parallels.

Psalm 22:18	"They have parted my garments among them, and for my vesture have cast lots."
Luke 23:34b:	"And they cast lots to divide his garments."
Psalm 22:7–8:	"All that see me have laughed me to scorn; they said with their lips while they shook their head: He trusted in the Lord, let him deliver him; let him save him, since he delights in him."
Wisdom 2:18:	"For if the righteous man is God's son, he will help him, and will deliver him from the hand of his adversaries."
Luke 23:35:	"And the people stood by, watching; but the rulers scoffed at him, saying, 'He saved others; let him save himself, if he is the Christ of God, his Chosen One!' "
Psalm 69:21:	"They indeed have given me gall for my food, and for my thirst, have made me drink vinegar."
Luke 23:36:	"The soldier mocked him, coming up and offering him vinegar."
Psalm 31:5:	"Into thy hands I will commit my spirit. You, O Lord, the God of truth, have redeemed me."
Luke 23:46:	"Then Jesus, crying with a loud voice, said, 'Father, into thy hands I commit my spirit!' "
Psalm 38:11:	"My friends and my neighbors stood over against me; they drew near and halted; even my close relations stood aloof."
Luke 23:49:	"And all his acquaintances and the women who had followed him from Galilee stood at a distance and saw these things."

In our treatment of the themes of poor and temptation which follow, we will have opportunity to explore in greater detail the significance of these parallels. At this juncture, one major observation will suffice. This sequence of passages on the innocently suffering righteous one accords with what we have seen of this theme in Luke 1–22. And it also accords with what Luke will say about this theme via the title of the Just One in Acts 3:14 (Peter's sermon), 7:52 (Stephen's address), and 22:14 (Paul's speech). See, e.g., Acts 22:14: "And Ananias said, 'The God of our fathers appointed you to know his will, to see the Just One and to hear a voice from his mouth.' " In Luke 23:34b–39 and in the rest of Luke's Gospel we have the narrative presentation of what is shown in the title of "Jesus the Just One" in Luke's second volume, The Acts of the Apostles. What makes this observation important at this point of our argument is that it shows that God will vindicate his innocently suffering Just One, Jesus. In Luke's story in Acts of how the church is led out onto the highways of universalism by Jesus, the Just One, Paul is converted from persecuting the church which continues Jesus' justice mission. He is converted by seeing the Just One, Jesus, whom God has raised from his unjust death. The attentive reader will not fail to notice that Paul is converted by "seeing" the Just One. Paul sees in faith that God has not abandoned his righteous Son, Jesus, but was with him in and through death. This motif of seeing occurs in 23:35 in the passage under consideration and again in 23:47–49.

Poor

It is quite obvious that in Luke 23 the word "poor" does not occur. Nevertheless, I maintain that the theme of poor is present although specific words for poor are not present. This thematic is present in the broader theme of the suffering righteous one. In his analyses of the materials on the innocently suffering righteous one, Lothar Ruppert has made a strong case that mix-and-match terms are involved. That is, on one level "righteous" is contrasted with "ungodly"; "poor" is contrasted with "wealthy"; and "lowly" is contrasted with "proud." But on another level, "righteous" is interchangeable with "poor" and "lowly." And "ungodly" is interchangeable with "wealthy" and "proud."[32] If Ruppert is correct, then Jesus, the innocently suffering righteous one, is also the poor one. Thus, with the death on the cross of Jesus, the righteous one (23:47), the Lukan theme of poor comes to a certain fullness of expression. Through the death and vindication of Jesus, the righteous and poor one, God has exalted those of low degree and filled the hungry with good things. God will never abandon the cause of those poor who, like Jesus, preach and live out God's good news to the poor.

Food and Clothing

There is no need to expand greatly on these themes. Sufficient on the theme of clothing, which occurs in 23:34b under the rubric of nakedness, is to remind the reader of what we said about clothing in our discussion of Luke 23:6–12. Jesus, the condemned prisoner, is stripped naked. By means of such humiliation he has lost his identity. On the symbolic level Jesus' nakedness shouts forth that this King, Christ, and Savior is a nobody. If readers are to attune themselves to the wavelength of this powerful symbol, they will have to shake themselves loose from the puritan attitude which fabricated the idea that the Romans would allow a loincloth on the Jewish crucified lest Jewish sensitivities be offended.

In Chapter Four we spent much time in Luke's kitchen as we pursued his theme of food. The Jesus who had enjoyed food so much and who had brought God's communion to outcasts by breaking bread with them is now given vinegar (23:36). The one who preached an alien God by being at table with sinners and thereby merited the condemnation as "a glutton and a drunkard" (7:34) is foodless and is given the drink of the innocently suffering righteous one. Is God or the power of darkness in control of food and life? Luke 23:43 will give the answer.

The People Are Watching;
The Religious Leaders Are Scoffing

Luke 23:35 shows us the stark contrast between the people who are watching and the religious leaders who are scoffing. The people, representative of those who are still open to God's kingly rule in Jesus, are on their way to conversion (see 23:48). They contemplate the events which surround Jesus' cross. The religious leaders, types of the closed and self-centered, are not open to see. As at 16:14, they scoff at the poor Jesus and his message.

Temptation

Luke's streamlining of Jesus' revilers into three distinct groups allows the reader to see more clearly how the three temptations of 23:34b–39 repeat the three of 4:1–13. Again the parallel to the righteous one of Wisdom 2:19 is apt: "Let us test him with insult and torture, that we may find out how gentle he is, and make trial of his forbearance." And as Luke has shown since the beginning of Luke 23, Jesus is a person of utmost integrity. Nothing, not even the salvation of his own physical existence, can lure him to disobey his Father God, whose plan for creation and humanity is coming to fulfillment in his own life. In his steadfast trust in God, Jesus is the living embodiment of his teaching in 12:1–34, especially 12:4–7: "I tell you, my friends, do not fear those who kill the body, and after that have no more that they can do. But I will warn you whom to fear: fear him who, after he has killed, has power to cast into hell; yes, I tell you, fear him! Are not five sparrows sold for two pennies? And not one of them is forgotten before God. Why, even the hairs of your head are all numbered. Fear not; you are of more value than many sparrows."

Christology and Soteriology

Besides the majestic portrayal of God's desire to be with his estranged creation in the person of Jesus, the obedient and innocently suffering righteous one, there are other aspects of christology and soteriology present in this passage. In the irony of the mockery Jesus is really all that he is taunted with: he is the Christ of God (22:35, 9:20). He is God's Chosen One (23:35; 9:35). He is King (23:37–38; 19:38). And as so many of the stories of Jesus' mighty deeds have shown, he is Savior from all the powers, be they sicknesses, the forces of chaos, or death itself, which enslave humanity. These titles, found ironically on the lips of Jesus' revilers, recapitulate what earlier portions of the Gospel have said that Jesus truly is.

There is still another dimension to Luke's christology present in this passage. It deals with Jesus as the person of trust who has faith in the faithfulness of the God who is leading him on the journey to himself. This dimension is found in the verb "save" (*sōzō*). When the railers ask Jesus to "save himself," should we not translate the Greek verb *sōzō* the way we have throughout the Gospel with "heal, rescue, save"? On one level, 23:35–39 is describing a deathly sick Jesus who is being jeered at as one who healed others, but cannot heal himself. And what has healed these other folks? Their faith! See, e.g., 17:19 and 18:42. Jesus' faith will heal/save/rescue him from the hands of evil and place him in the hands of the faithful God.

In brief, 23:34b–39 is richly laden with beautifully powerful Lukan themes. As Luke's kerygmatic story of Jesus comes to an end, we grasp more fully how Luke's themes have enabled him to grant assurance to his faithful readers (see Luke 1:1–4). The God, visible in Jesus, wants to be and will be with them. The God in whom they believe will be faithful to them as he was to Jesus.

LUKE 23:40–43

⁴⁰But the other rebuked him, saying, 'Do you not fear God, since you are under the same sentence of condemnation? ⁴¹And we indeed justly; for we are receiving the due reward of our deeds; but this man has done nothing wrong.' ⁴²And he said, 'Jesus, remember me when you come in your kingly power.' ⁴³And he said to him, 'Truly, I say to you, today you will be with me in Paradise.'

This passage, unique to Luke, has oft been called the "Gospel within the Gospel." In many ways it is the narrative highpoint of the Gospel. We will sample the significance of the many themes which course through its verses.

Jesus as the Innocent Righteous One

Again Luke strikes the refrain of Jesus' innocence. To the voices of Pilate and Herod Luke adds that of the repentant malefactor: "And we indeed justly; for we are receiving the due reward of our deeds; but this man has done nothing wrong" (23:41). Obedient to his Father's will and a person of integrity amidst the temptations of 23:34b–39, Jesus is the innocently suffering righteous one. Through his innocent death issues life for repentant outcasts.

God's Kingdom Is for Outcasts

Ever since 19:11 Luke has struck with vigor the theme of Jesus the king. At the nadir of his physical power Jesus exercises his vast power as king at the request of an outcast, the repentant malefactor (23:42–43). Salvation for this individual, who represents all repentant evil-doers, is not in the future. As Jesus had demonstrated time and again during his ministry of word and deed, God's kingdom is effective in the present. And what is most striking in this passage is that that kingly power is exercised "today" by a dying savior. Through his death Jesus grants union with God to those whom society condemns.

Food and the Cross

As Chapter Four has shown in great detail, the aromas of food emanate from every chapter of Luke. In 23:43 they are at their attractive best.

The key to an analysis of 23:43 lies in the word "paradise," for in that word the themes of food, New Adam, and righteous ones are contained. J. Jeremias summarizes the food aspect of the image of paradise in this way: "Its (the reopened paradise) most important gifts are the fruits of the tree of life, the water and bread of life, the banquet of salvation, and fellowship with God."[33] What had been lost by Adam and Eve has now been restored to men and women. The symbols, which we explored in Chapter Four above, all come together via the symbol of paradise. Through his death Jesus gives repentant men and women life, represented by "the fruits of the tree of life." They live by the fruits which come from the new tree of life, the cross of Jesus.[34] The bread, which Jesus shared so often with others as he nurtured them, now comes from his cross. The messianic banquet, imaged by Jesus in his joyful table fellowship with tax collectors and sinners, is reality through his death.

Although Luke does not say so in so many words, his image of paradise readily lends itself to the view that Jesus is the New Adam. Again Jeremias is right on target: "What really matters is not the felicity of

Paradise but the restoration of the communion with God which was broken by Adam's fall."[35] As the one who has restored the communion with God which was broken by Adam's fall, Jesus is the New Adam. Unlike Adam, who succumbed to temptations, Jesus, the New Adam, does not (see 23:34b–39). Obedient to God's will to the end, Jesus opens up the path to life for all men and women.

Finally, the symbol of paradise rejoins us to the theme of the righteous ones. Again as Jeremias has shown, paradise is the place for the righteous.[36] Jesus, the righteous one par excellence, has the keys to the home of the righteous. He not only is righteous himself, but goes against the norms of society and declares a malefactor fit for the place for the righteous.

To recapitulate, the theme of food pulses powerfully through 23:40–43. The powers of darkness and human perversity cannot and will not prevent God from giving food to his creation. Through Jesus' life and especially through his death God is in control of food. God gives life to creation and humanity. The powers arrayed against God's righteous ones will not succeed in starving them to death.[37]

The Winsome Nature of the Good Malefactor

The "good malefactor" is a carrier of three Lukan motifs. The word "rebuke" (23:40) introduces us to the first motif. The "good malefactor" manifests one of the characteristics of discipleship by "rebuking" the sinner. See 17:3 wherein the same Greek word, translated by "rebuke," occurs: "Take heed to yourselves; if your brother sins, rebuke him, and if he repents, forgive him."

The "good evil-doer" is also an embodiment of the faith and trust which characterize the disciple. The three groups of tempters in 23:34b–39 know the correct titles of Jesus: Christ of God, Chosen one, and King, but do not have faith in Jesus. The plea of the "good malefactor" is shot through with the faith that saves: "Jesus, remember me when you come in your kingly power" (23:42).

The word "Jesus" (23:42) sets us along the right path in our pursuit of the third Lukan motif found in this passage. The honorific titles given to Jesus in 23:34b–39 contrast sharply with the simple name, Jesus, voiced by the "good evil-doer." This name is unique in the context. But as Acts 4:12 shows, solely in the name of Jesus is there salvation: "And there is salvation in no one else, for there is no other name under heaven given among men by which we must be saved.'' A name means all that stands behind the person who bears that name. In the case of Jesus it is his entire kingdom mission as God's prophet and righteous one. All appearances to the contrary notwithstanding, the crucified Jesus does save because God stands behind his ''name'' and will not allow his righteous one and those who believe in his name to see corruption.

Luke's Thematic Christology and Soteriology

In the gospel in miniature of 23:40–43, the theme of Jesus, the righteous one who proclaims in word and by life-style that God's kingly justice is for the outcasts, comes to a fullness of narrative articulation as Jesus invites a condemned malefactor into paradise. The theme of Jesus, God's food for humankind, finds a fullness of expression as Jesus gifts the malefactor with life beyond death at the banquet of the righteous. The theme of Jesus, who scandalizes the so-called righteous by joyously eating and drinking with the unrighteous, enters upon a fullness of expression as Jesus, the faithful prophet, promises the ''good malefactor'' that he will be *with* him at the banquet of life. That Jesus does all this—activities befitting God and his dealings with humankind—expresses his relationship with his faithful God. That he does all this expresses his power to save. Through his death Jesus restores a fallen and estranged humanity to communion with God.

LUKE 23:44–45

[44]It was now about the sixth hour, and there was darkness over the whole land until the ninth hour, [45]while the sun's light failed; and the curtain of the temple was torn in two.

Darkness

There are two motifs in Luke 23:44–45: darkness and temple. It is important to realize that Luke does not say that the darkness was a natural phenomenon, due to an eclipse of the sun.[38] It is also important to recall that he has used darkness earlier in a symbolic way: in 22:53 he described Jesus' embarkation on the road to crucifixion as a result of the "powers of darkness." Thus, we will not be surprised to find that Luke uses "darkness" in 23:44–45 in a symbolic or thematic way.

As we have seen earlier, it is a Lukan characteristic to employ symbols and themes which are meaningful in both Graeco-Roman and Jewish cultures.[39] Relative to the Graeco-Roman background for the theme of darkness, Charles H. Talbert is quite informative:

> In the Greco-Roman mentality events with cosmic significance were attested by cosmic signs (e.g., Lucan, *Civil War* 7:199–200, says that at the battle of Pharsalia the 'sorrowing deity in heaven gave notice of the battle by the dimness and obscurity of the sun'). This was a time of the power of darkness (22:53).[40]

The tragedy of Jesus' unjust crucifixion on earth is of such global significance that heaven itself attests to its import.

In Jewish milieux the failure of the sun was often associated with the act of God's deliverance from injustice as God fulfilled the hopes of Israel. One of the prime Old Testament witnesses for this motif is Joel 2:31, which is the backbone for Luke's fulfillment theology in Acts 2:20. Joel 2:31 reads: "The sun shall be turned into darkness and the moon into blood before the great and terrible day of the Lord comes" (New English Bible). The terrible day of the Lord, that is, the day on which God fulfills his promises by vindicating those who are oppressed, begins in Luke with Jesus' crucifixion and continues to the Pentecost event of the sending of the promised Spirit (Acts 2).

A second vital witness for the Jewish flavor of the motif of darkness is Amos 8:9. It should be recalled that this verse occurs in the context of Amos' prophecies about injustices against the poor and needy (Amos 8:4–6). God will vindicate his justice and care for the oppressed, as the prophet confesses: "On that day, says the Lord God, I will make the sun go down at noon and darken the earth in broad daylight" (New English Bible). In Luke's presentation the eschatological day, "the day of the Lord," dawns with Jesus' death. God is fulfilling his promises of life for the oppressed as he darkens the earth during the broad daylight of noon. "The day of the Lord" is not in some unimaginable future, but is seen today. And it is seen in the most unlikely of places, in a crucified person, Jesus of Nazareth.

The motif of darkness reacquaints us with the major Lukan motif of the faithful God. The God who seems to have been unfaithful to his promises and unfaithful to his innocently suffering righteous ones, typified in Jesus, is fulfilling his promises in the face of the power of death. In and through the "darkness" this faithful God is liberating the oppressed.

Temple

Behind the short sentence, "and the curtain of the temple was torn in two" (23:45), stands Luke's motif of the temple. It is impossible to delve into this motif here. A few general directives will have to suffice. In our passage the reference is to the curtain which separates worshipers from the Holy of Holies, God's very presence. A second key point is one which Francis D. Weinert has been reminding us of, namely, along with the many Lukan passages which predict the destruction of the temple, there are those, especially in Acts, which speak positively of the temple.[41] In brief, it is inadequate to read Luke 23:45 simply as another reference to the destruction of the temple. Finally, the reference to the torn temple curtain must be read in conjunction with the verse that follows which expresses Jesus' total dedication to God. More detail on the importance of Luke 23:46 will be provided in the next section.

With these general directions in mind, I would express the meaning of the motif of temple thusly. The temple motif does indeed function positively, helping Luke express the continuity between the Christian Way and God's covenantal promises to Israel. It helps him develop his view of the "restored Israel." But the temple is also being replaced by Jesus. This Lukan view is perhaps expressed most graphically in Acts 22:17–21 which describes the appearance of Jesus to Paul in the temple. In a religious world which was fond of telling stories of how the god of the temple appeared to devotees in his temple, Luke is saying in effect that Jesus is the God of the temple. And the powerful story of Acts 22:17–21 is anticipated by Luke 23:45: the God of the temple, whose presence was veiled by the temple curtain, is now seen in Jesus. The one whose first recorded words in Luke's Gospel were spoken in the temple: "Did you not know that I must be in my Father's house?" (2:49), now is his Father's house as he dies revealing God's kingly power. Not only has the Lord come into his temple (2:22–41), he is the temple now.

Women and men find God's self-disclosure not behind the Holy of Holies of the temple, but in Jesus.

As we will see below in detail, the pagan centurion sees these things (23:47). The pagan, at Jesus' death, finds himself within the Holy of Holies, in the presence of God. He praises the mighty deed of God's presence in a crucified person. Pagans need not worship at the temple of Apollo or Isis, for the God of sun and earth is present in the temple of Jesus, an innocently suffering righteous one.

LUKE 23:46

⁴⁶Then Jesus, crying with a loud voice, said, 'Father, into thy hands I commit my spirit!' And having said this, he breathed his last.

It is a commonplace observation to say that death separates us from the experiences of the beauty of creation, loved ones, and God. Many people at the time of Luke expressed this observation on their tombstones with: "I was not, I am not, I don't give a damn!" (*Non fui, non sum, non curo.*) In his kerygmatic narrative of Jesus' death Luke challenges this commonplace observation with the perspective of Jesus' faith in his faithful God.

The Faith of Jesus, the Innocently Suffering Righteous One

In our discussion of Luke 23:34b–39 we laid out the many Old Testament allusions to the theme of the innocently suffering righteous one found in those verses. We also pointed ahead to 23:46, which is derived almost word for word from Psalm 31:5: "Into thy hands I will commit my spirit. Thou, O Lord, the God of truth, hast redeemed me." Jesus' life ends with a prayer of trust in the God who redeems the innocently suffering righteous ones. Jesus' prayer anticipates Luke's account of Jesus' resurrection and exaltation which will fully demonstrate God's unconditional will to save his crippled and wayward creation. Despite the lure of human perversity so prominently displayed during his crucifixion, Jesus remains faithful to God, whom he trusts as forever faithful.

Jesus is the poor person par excellence, totally dependent upon God, totally obedient to God's will and plan. Confident that the hands into which he commits his life are gracious, he completes his journey of faith. From the inception of his ministry Jesus has been portrayed as walking the path of justice, challenging the self-exalting life-style of the righteous. To his last words Jesus will not exalt himself. As God's righteous one, God's Son, Jesus is completely dedicated to God to the end. He is the leader on the journey, as he opens up the way of faith. As Acts will say, Jesus is the leader who has broken through the power of darkness into God's realm: "But you denied the Holy and Righteous One, and asked for a murderer to be granted to you, and killed the Author of life, whom God raised from the dead" (Acts 3:15).

From time to time people have raised the question of how a dying crucified person could "cry with a loud voice." This is a good question on the level of the historical reliability of Luke's account and provides an excellent introduction to the theme being carried by "with a loud voice." In Luke "with a loud voice" indicates the presence of the divine, e.g., 8:28; 19:37. Two responses are possible: to run away from the divine in fear or to praise, thank, and trust the divine. The phrase, "with a loud voice," is used only in 23:46 of Jesus. In and through death, the ultimate enemy, Jesus experiences the presence of God. And "with a loud voice" he praises God, the giver and sustainer of life, and trusts that God will not withdraw the gift of that life. He trusts that God and not death control the food of life. He trusts that God is Father, giver of life.

The Faithful God

Much of what should be said about the theme of the faithful God is closely tied to the theme of Jesus, the righteous one, and has already been stated in the previous paragraphs. A few additional comments will suffice.

The key observation about the theme of the faithful God is one which we have frequently made: the nature of God is to be with his creation. This with-ness characteristic of God comes to a certain fullness of expression in 23:46. Through his fidelity to Jesus whom he called to journey to himself, God shows forth his will to be with men and women even in their darkest and most dire hours, even in the throes of an unjust death. Death, the ultimate enemy of creation, does not separate men and women from the faithful God. Through the death of Jesus, who dies prayerfully confident of God's vindication/redemption, God shows that he is with his creation.

The dying Jesus reveals a God in whom one can trust, one who is trustworthy. And as contemporary research on the phenomenon of trust is indicating, trust is a mutual gift.[42] We do not force someone to trust us. We are gifted with trust in another person. The theme of the trust of the innocently suffering righteous one, Jesus, reveals another aspect of the Lukan soteriology. God grants salvation wholly gratuitously to those who trust in his graciousness as Jesus did. The God at the end of the journey of humankind is gracious.

In conclusion, Jesus' dying prayer in 23:46 should be linked to his other words in 23:28,31,34,43, all of which show his unity with his Father's will to save humankind, even in its darkest hours. The centurion of 23:47 will praise this righteous God at work in Jesus' death.

LUKE 23:47-49

[47]Now when the centurion saw what had taken place, he praised God, and said, 'Certainly this man was innocent/righteous!' [48]And all the multitudes who assembled to see the sight, when they saw what had taken place, returned home beating their breasts. [49]And all his acquaintances and the women who had followed him from Galilee stood at a distance and saw these things.

In what follows we will explore the reactions of individuals to the events of Jesus' last hours. Since one of the primary Lukan vehicles for depicting these reactions is the theme of "seeing," I invite the reader to check back over what I said about this theme in the section on Luke 23:7–12 above.

The Seeing of the Pagan Centurion

Four points are important in 23:47, and we are put on their trail by the skeptic's question: "If it were dark, how could the centurion see what had taken place?" It seems reasonable to say that "what had taken place" goes back in the story to 23:26 when the centurion and his soldiers led Jesus away. Thus, what the centurion has seen take place would include: Jesus' prayer for forgiveness of his enemies; Jesus' integrity amidst the temptations to save himself; Jesus' power to grant the banquet of life to a malefactor; the darkness of God's presence at Jesus' death; Jesus as the God of the temple whose curtain is torn in two; God as the trustworthy Father of his innocently suffering righteous one.

Seeing these things, the centurion "praised God." With the phrase "to praise God" Luke connects Jesus' last hours with his theme of God's mighty deeds. For in Luke "to praise God" is a response to a revelation of God's power and mercy present in a mighty deed (see, e.g., Luke 2:20; 5:25,26; 7:16; 13:13; 17:15; 18:43; 23:47; Acts 4:21; 21:20). Unlike Herod, who out of curiosity wanted to see a mighty deed of Jesus (23:8), the pagan centurion does see a mighty deed of God. But that mighty deed does not occur in raising a dead man to life (7:16), or in healing a leper (17:15), or in giving sight to the blind (18:43). That mighty deed, that revelation of God's power and mercy, occurs in the death of a crucified person, Jesus of Nazareth. There is God's power and mercy—to be with his unjustly treated creation in and through death, to lavish choice food on an evil-doer, to forgive enemies. Jesus, who in his nakedness has no apparent identity, is God's revelation. And the centurion praises the God thus revealed.

Our third significant point has surfaced already in the discussion of "what had taken place" and "praised God." It is the theme of seeing, a Lukan and biblical expression for receiving God's revelation (see, e.g., Luke 1:78–79; 2:32; 9:27; 10:18,23–24; Acts 22:12–15; 26:16–23). The pagan centurion sees with the eyes of faith the central significance of Jesus. His faith is pure gift. This pagan teams up with the Jewish malefactor of 23:40–43 to show forth in narrative form the universalism of God's kingdom message in Jesus.

The final observation about 23:47 concerns the centurion's confession. The centurion says that Jesus was *dikaios*. This Greek word can mean "innocent" or "righteous." Translated as "innocent," it accords well with the motif of Jesus as the condemned innocent one (see 23:4,14,22). Translated as "righteous," it accords well with the overriding Lukan motif of God's righteousness and Jesus as the righteous one. And as we have seen time and again in our commentary on Luke 23, that theme streams powerfully through this chapter. Rather than get trapped in an either-or dead-end discussion, let us say that the Greek adjective *dikaios* means both "innocent" and "righteous" in 23:47. Both meanings are well captured in the phrase I have been employing throughout our consideration of Luke 23: innocently suffering righteous one.

With that translation vagary behind us, we can concentrate on the meaning of the centurion's confession. As we have seen, the centurion is saying more than "Jesus was an innocent martyr." While the centurion's profession is not that same as that found in Mark and Matthew— Jesus is the Son of God—his confession is nevertheless high christology. Jesus is righteous as he manifests his probity in the face of his adversaries. God shows himself to be righteous by being faithful to his unjustly treated creation, thematized in Jesus as the innocently suffering righteous one. By being righteous, Jesus has shown that he is God's Son. By being faithful and righteous to Jesus, God has shown that Jesus is his Son. As Wisdom 2:18 eloquently puts the logic of the theme of God's righteous one: "For if the righteous man is God's son, he will help him, and will deliver him from the hand of his adversaries." As the subsequent narrative of Jesus' resurrection and exaltation will show, God had indeed vindicated his righteous Jesus from the hand of his adversaries. Death and the powers of injustice cannot deter the righteous God from the fulfillment of his plan for humankind.

In brief, Luke 23:47 dramatizes many of the key Lukan motifs and leads into two additional verses which deal with "seeing."

The People Who See and Repent

Before we commence our brief comments on Luke 23:48, I would invite my readers to review what I said about "the people" in Chapter Three above in our discussion of Luke 7:29–30. It would also be helpful for my readers to glance back over my remarks in this chapter about Luke 23:13–25. In 23:48 Luke's normal usage is to be presupposed: "multitudes" is equivalent to "crowd," and both are equivalent to "the people." Thus, the people whom Luke depicted in 23:13–25 as demanding Jesus' crucifixion and in 23:35 as watching how he died now respond to Jesus' death.

Luke 23:35 tipped us readers off that the people's denial of Jesus, described so poignantly in 23:13–25, did not shut them down to further manifestations of God's kingdom in Jesus. Unlike the religious leaders who scoff at Jesus, the people assume a more positive attitude and watch. And Luke will not let us forget this posture, for he thrice refers to seeing in 23:48. And what did the people see? Since they beat their breasts as a sign of repentance (see 18:13), their sight must be one of depth, of faith. With the eyes of faith they have seen in Jesus the same things take place which the centurion did—with one exception. In addition to what the pagan centurion saw, they have seen his conversion as evidenced in his confession of faith in Jesus as God's righteous one.

The open and watchful people, who had attentively and positively followed Jesus from the beginnings of his Galilean ministry of justice and had momentarily shut down their quest for God under pressure, now beat their breasts. As the parallel in Luke 18:13 suggests, to beat one's breast is a sign of repentance. What they have seen of the faithful God's activities during Jesus' last moments has led them to faith and repentance.

Space limitations dictate that our remarks on the large Lukan motif of repentance, which is broached in 23:48, be few here. The repentance motif, sounded in 23:48 and heard often in Luke, must not be taken in some pietistic sense and thus reduced to the sentimental ''I'm sorry that I have crucified the Lord Jesus who loves me so much.'' Luke's story of Jesus and the people goes back to Jesus' Galilean ministry and suggests that their repentance is not something which occurs spontaneously. Rather it is based upon reflection about Jesus' kingdom mission. Repentance in Luke is to see that God is revealed in Jesus' ministry of justice. It is to lay oneself open to the claims of that God, whose will for humankind is revealed in Jesus' scandalous table fellowship with sinners. It is to trust in the faithful God and not in mammon. In sum, it is to let one's life be nurtured by Jesus' vision of the faithful God who in Jesus' death shows that he has defeated death, the final obstacle to communion with men and women.

Jesus' Acquaintances and Faithful Women Disciples See

As I pointed out in our discussion of Luke 23:34b–39 above, there is some slight possibility that Luke 23:49 is an allusion to Psalm 38:11, one of the psalms of the innocently suffering righteous one: ''My friends and my neighbors stood over against me; they drew near and halted; even my close relations stood aloof.'' But the allusion does not seem to be present, for whereas Psalm 38:11 is largely negative, Luke 23:49 has a largely positive view of those who are around the dying Jesus. Jesus' acquaintances and women disciples do not abandon him.

Much of the positive meaning of 23:49 is to be found in Luke's motif of witness. Again only a few general remarks on this motif are permitted us. If you recall, Luke does not say that all Jesus' disciples fled away from him on the Mount of Olives. Also Luke does not say that Peter denied Jesus; he says rather that Peter denied that he knew Jesus. Behind "all his acquaintances" in 23:49 stands a reference to the apostles, who have not abandoned Jesus. They are present at the cross as witnesses. In Luke's account these are the prime witnesses of the Gospel (see especially Acts 1:21–22).[43] The faithful women disciples who have followed Jesus from Galilee also witness Jesus' last hours. The dual witness of the male apostles and the faithful women disciples touches base with another Lukan theme—the universality of the Gospel which knows no gender boundaries.[44]

And what Luke means by "witness" is signaled by "saw these things." Their witness is not mere physical presence to the events and seeing with physical eyes. It is witness, informed by the sight of faith. They see what the centurion and what the multitudes/crowd/the people see. And their seeing provides Luke with a bridge to Chapter 24, for in that chapter Luke gives full theological and thematic play to his motif of seeing. The risen Lord Jesus opens the eyes of both men and women disciples to see that all God's kingdom promises have come to fulfillment in him. In Jesus the faithful God has conquered death and shares again the kingdom meal of forgiveness and communion. It is to this faithful God that the disciples will give witness as they are sent on mission to all nations.

In resume of Luke 23:47–49, let us change the focus of the motif of "seeing" a little. Men and women are invited to see their brothers and sisters and God through the eyes of the crucified Jesus, who forgives the enemy, trusts in the goodness of a convicted malefactor, and commits himself to a God who communes with his unjustly treated creatures. Truly, the events narrated in Luke 23:35–49 are worth contemplation.

LUKE 23:50–56

[50]Now there was a man named Joseph from the Jewish town of Arimathea. He was a member of the council, a good and right-

eous man, [51]who had not consented to their purpose and deed, and he was looking for the kingdom of God. [52]This man went to Pilate and asked for the body of Jesus. [53]Then he took it down and wrapped it in a linen shroud, and laid him in a rock-hewn tomb, where no one had ever yet been laid. [54]It was the day of Preparation, and the sabbath was beginning. [55]The women who had come with him from Galilee followed, and saw the tomb, and how his body was laid; [56]then they returned, and prepared spices and ointments. On the sabbath they rested according to the commandment.

Luke began Chapter 23 with a reference to the council. Now he ends it with a reference to the council. And as we observed in our treatment of 23:1–5, there is tension between statements made there and those made here in 23:50–54. Whereas Luke 22:70 and 23:1 state quite clearly that all members of the council were against Jesus, 23:50–54 accents Joseph of Arimathea as the exception. This singular reference to a righteous religious leader shows that Luke does not use the motif of the unrighteous religious leaders to give a thoroughgoing negative view of the human condition.

Joseph of Arimathea is the embodiment of discipleship: one who pursues a justice way of life and who is responsive to God's kingly rule in Jesus of Nazareth (23:50–51). Luke 23:53 seems to suggest that Joseph of Arimathea buried Jesus in his own tomb. An unused tomb in Jerusalem was a prized possession. As a genuine disciple, Joseph of Arimathea gives up his possessions for the sake of Jesus. In brief, in the person of Joseph of Arimathea we encounter a representative example of what it means to be righteous.

In our exploration of the meaning of 23:6–12 we gave a short tour of the theme of clothing. That theme reappears in 23:53. The naked Jesus is clothed in linen, the symbol of immortality, in the hope that God will raise him from the dead. That hope finds narrative and thematic fulfillment in 24:12: Peter sees the linen clothes by themselves. The symbol of resurrection life has given way to the reality of the risen Jesus, who symbolizes what God has planned for all his creation.

In 23:55–56 we once again encounter Jesus' women disciples, who have faithfully followed him from Galilee. In these verses Luke not only stresses the steadfastness of discipleship, but also prepares for 24:1–11 which contains a climax for his theme of women. A close study of 24:1–11, especially the "remembering" motif of 24:6–9, would show that in Luke women are the first ones given the mission of proclaiming the resurrection faith. It is not their fault, but rather a sign of the denseness of human perception that the men do not believe them.

CONCLUSION TO CHAPTER FIVE

We have traveled a long way in this chapter. A summary is needful, lest the essentials of Luke's christology and soteriology be lost in haystacks of detail. Luke's kerygmatic narrative has frequently riveted our attention on Luke's functional christology. For example, in his joyous communion at table with outcasts the Lukan Jesus has embodied God's kingly mercy by performing the actions of a faithful God who wants to be united with his creation. In Chapter 23 Luke continues to describe Jesus, the man of utmost integrity and obedience, as one who effects God's deeds, especially the deed of granting entry into the banquet of paradise to those deemed least worthy of such gratuitous consideration.

Luke maintains that God saves in Jesus from sin and death, the powers that separate men and women from one another and from God. But he does not argue his case with the imagery of Jesus' expiatory death for sin. His argument consists primarily of the themes of God's righteousness, faith, and journey. By granting the life of the resurrection to the innocently crucified righteous one, Jesus, who typifies God's creation held in the power of sin and death, God shows that he, and not the powers of chaos, is righteous king. God reigns over sin and death; God saves. And in Luke's narrative God's saving action in Jesus' life, death, and exaltation must be accepted by "seeing" with faith. Salvific faith is personal trust in a God who is ultimately faithful to his promises of life. Furthermore, the believer, addressed by Luke (see Luke 1:1–4), has a model of faith in Jesus, the righteous one, whose journey to God was traversed along the road of justice. Jesus has opened the way to God and invites men and women to journey to God along his way of justice, confident that God has conquered the powers which might undermine that journey and prevent union with him.

NOTES

1. "Eléments artistiques," 138.

2. On recent developments in the scholarly study of Luke's soteriology, see Richard, "Luke," 6.

3. As occasion warrants, bibliography on these Lukan themes will be provided. See, in general, Navone, *Themes.*

4. Detailed exegesis can be found in the standard commentaries. In this chapter my thinking has been informed and stimulated by the following works, for which I here provide full bibliographical data, even for those works previously cited, in order to aid the interested reader: C.K. Barrett, "Theologia Crucis—in Acts?" in *Theologia Crucis—Signum Crucis: Festschrift fuer Erich Dinkler zum 70. Geburtstag* (ed. C. Andresen; G. Klein; Tuebingen: Mohr, 1979) 73–84; Brian E. Beck, "*'Imitatio Christi'* and the Lucan Passion Narrative," in *Suffering and Martyrdom in the New Testament: Studies presented to G.M. Styler by the Cambridge New Testament Seminar* (ed. William Horburg; Brian McNeil; Cambridge: Cambridge University, 1981) 28–47; François Bovon, *Luc le theologien: Vingt-cinq ans de recherches (1950–1975)* (Neuchatel/ Paris: Delachaux & Niestlé, 1978) 175–81; Anton Buechele, *Der Tod Jesu im Lukasevangelium: Eine redaktionsgeschichtliche Untersuchung zu Lk 23* (Frankfurter Theologische Studien 26; Frankfurt am Main: Josef Knecht, 1978); Jerome Crowe, "The Laos at the Cross: Luke's Crucifixion Scene," *The Language of the Cross* (ed. Aelred Lacomara; Chicago: Franciscan Herald, 1977) 75–101; Richard J. Dillon, *From Eye-Witnesses to Ministers of the Word: Tradition and Composition in Luke 24* (AnBib 82; Rome: Biblical Institute, 1978); Ludger Feldkaemper, *Der betende Jesus als Heilsmittler nach Lukas* (Veroeffentlichungen des Missionspriesterseminars St. Augustin bei Bonn 29; St. Augustin: Steyler, 1978); Augustin George, "Le sens de la mort de Jesus pour Luc," *RB* 80 (1973) 186–217; Richard Gloeckner, *Die Verkuendigung des Heils beim Evangelisten Lukas* (Walberberger Studien, Theologische Reihe 9; Mainz: Gruenwald, n.d. [1976], esp. pp. 155–95; Jerome Kodell, "Luke's Theology of the Death of Jesus," *Sin, Salvation, and the Spirit: Commemorating the Fiftieth Year of The Liturgical Press* (ed. Daniel Durken; Collegeville: Liturgical, 1979) 221–30; Jerome Kodell, "Luke's Use of *Laos,* 'People,' Especially in the Jerusalem Narrative (Lk 19,28–24,53)," *CBQ* 31 (1969) 327–43; Jerome H. Neyrey, "Jesus' Address to the Women of Jerusalem (Lk. 23.27–31)—A Prophetic Judgment Oracle," *NTS* 29 (1983) 74–86; Lothar Ruppert, *Jesus als der leidende Gerechte? Der Weg Jesu im Lichte eines alt- und zwischentestamentlichen Motivs* (SBS 59; Stuttgart: KBW, 1972); Lothar Ruppert, *Der leidende Gerechte: Eine motivgeschichtliche Untersuchung zum Alten Testament und zwischentestamentlichen Judentum* (Forschung zur Bibel 5; Wuerz-

burg: Echter/Stuttgart, KBW, 1972); Lothar Ruppert, *Der leidende Gerechte und seine Feinde: Eine Wortfelduntersuchung* (Wuerzburg: Echter, 1973); Gerhard Schneider, *Verleugnung, Verspottung und Verhoer Jesu nach Lukas 22,54–71* (SANT 22; Munich: Koesel, 1969), esp. pp. 174–210; David L. Tiede, *Prophecy and History in Luke-Acts* (Philadelphia: Fortress, 1980); Franz Georg Untergassmair, *Kreuzweg und Kreuzigung Jesu: Ein Beitrag zur lukanischen Redaktionsgeschichte und zur Frage nach der lukanischen "Kreuzestheologie"* (Paderborner Theologische Studien 10; Paderborn: Schoeningh, 1980); Franz Georg Untergassmair, "Thesen zur Sinndeutung des Todes Jesu in der lukanische Passionsgeschichte," *TGI* 70 (1980) 180–93; Albert Vanhoye, *Structure and Theology of the Accounts of the Passion in the Synoptic Gospels* (The Bible Today, Supplementary Studies 1; Collegeville: Liturgical, 1967); Paul W. Walaskay, "The Trial and Death of Jesus in the Gospel of Luke," *JBL* 94 (1975) 81–93; Hans-Ruedi Weber, *The Cross: Tradition and Interpretation* (Grand Rapids: Eerdmans, 1979) 117–24.

5. On the question of historicity, see the nuanced study by Gerard S. Sloyan, *Jesus on Trial: The Development of the Passion Narratives and Their Historical and Ecumenical Implications* (ed. with an Introduction by John Reumann; Philadelphia: Fortress, 1973).

6. The studies of George W.E. Nickelsburg might be applied to Luke's passion narrative. See his "The Genre and Function of the Markan Passion Narrative," *HTR* 73 (1980) 153–84, wherein he argues that the multiple motifs of the passion narrative should be set into a single literary genre: the story of persecution and vindication. However, the studies of Buechele and Untergassmair have convinced me that the perspective of "literary genre" does not do justice to the richness of Luke 23 which must be seen within the entire context of Luke of which it is an intimate part. See especially Untergassmair, *Kreuzweg und Kreuzigung Jesu*, 156–71.

7. See Robert Maddox, *The Purpose of Luke-Acts* (Studies of the New Testament and Its World; Edinburgh: T. & T. Clark, 1982) 158–79, esp. pp. 163–64.

8. See ibid., 91–99; see now Paul W. Walaskay, *'And so we came to Rome': The Political Perspective of St Luke* (SNTSMS 49; Cambridge: Cambridge University, 1983).

9. See Vincent Taylor, *The Passion Narrative of St Luke: A Critical and Historical Investigation* (ed. Owen E. Evans; SNTSMS 19; Cambridge: Cambridge University, 1972).

10. A helpful study on this Lukan motif of Jesus as king is: Luke T. Johnson, "The Lukan Kingship Parable (Lk. 19:11–27)," *NovT* 2 (1982) 139–59.

11. See Harold W. Hoehner, "Why Did Pilate Hand Jesus Over to Antipas?" in *The Trial of Jesus: Cambridge Studies in Honour of C.F.D. Moule* (ed.

Ernst Bammel; SBT 2/13; London: SCM, 1970) 84–90; Sloyan, *Jesus on Trial*, 100. For other theories on why Pilate sent Jesus to Herod or why they became friends after Jesus appeared before the tetrarch, see Walaskay, "The Trial and Death of Jesus," 87–90.

12. On this Lukan theme see John Drury, *Tradition and Design in Luke's Gospel: A Study in Early Christian Historiography* (Atlanta: John Knox, 1976) 17; Michel Corbin, "Jesus devant Herode: Lecture de *Luc* 23,6–12," *Christus* 25 (1978) 190–97.

13. See Donahue, "The Good News of Peace," 88–99.

14. *The Birth Of the Messiah*, 420.

15. *Luke*, 714.

16. *Symbolique du Vêtement selon la Bible* (Théologie 65; Paris: Aubier, 1966) 79.

17. Ibid., 79–89.

18. "A Pythagorean Idea in Jerome," *American Journal of Philology* 63 (1942) 206–15.

19. "Luc 23,11: *esthēta lampran*," *RSR* 26 (1936) 80–85.

20. See Luke 3:1,19; 9:7. Acts 4:25–27 is only an apparent exception.

21. See A. Oepke, *"Lampō, Ktl,"* *TDNT* 4.17; Harold W. Hoehner, *Herod Antipas* (SNTSMS 17; Cambridge: Cambridge University, 1972) 243 n. 1.

22. See James D.G. Dunn, *Baptism in the Holy Spirit* (Philadelphia: Westminster, 1970) 76–77.

23. See Dillon, *Eye-Witnesses*, 145–49, 217, 292 and passim.

24. Mark 15:21 and Matt 27:32 use the Greek verb *aggareuo*, which means "press into service, force, compel" (consult BADG). Luke uses the Greek verb *epilambanomai*. It is true that Luke can use *epilambanomai* in the meaning of "seize": Acts 16:19; 18:17; 21:30,33. It is also true that Luke in Luke 9:47; 14:4; Acts 9:27; 17:19; 23:19 uses *epilambanomai* in the positive sense of "lay friendly hands on" a person for healing or for recommendation.

25. See Talbert, *Reading Luke*, 220 for convincing reasons why Luke 23:34a is authentic.

26. Many commentators are dependent upon the article by J. Schneider, *"zylon,"* *TDNT* 5.38 for understanding *zylon* as wood. Among other difficulties, Schneider's interpretation depends upon reading the verse historically and upon using later rabbinic parallels.

27. And God will raise Jesus up from his tree, as Acts 5:30, 10:39, and 13:29 indicate. In those three passages tree means cross.

28. In Pauline terms, God justifies the ungodly.

29. On the theme of prayer see my *What Are They Saying About Luke and Acts?*, 74–83.

30. *Structure and Theology*, 34.

31. Translations of psalms are based on the Septuagint.

32. The Greek involved is: *dikaios—asebeis; ptōchos—ploutos; tapeinos—hypērephanos.*

33. *"Paradeisos," TDNT* 5.767.

34. See above on 23:27–34a and the fact that in Acts Luke refers to Jesus' cross as a tree.

35. *TDNT* 5.773.

36. Ibid., 771.

37. The attentive reader will have noticed that 23:43 does not explicitly mention food, New Adam, or righteous ones, and yet we claim that these themes are present. The reader is encouraged to refer back to Chapter One on "theme." In general, themes are carried by many other elements of the story than by identical words. Themes, like diamonds, are multifaceted.

38. See Marshall, *Luke*, 875: Luke is not guilty of an astronomical blunder since an eclipse is impossible during Passover time; the phrase means "merely that the sun failed to give its light (cf. Job 31:26; Is. 60:20; Sir. 22:11)."

39. Recall what we said above in Chapter Four during our discussion of Luke 14:1–24: the Lukan motifs of symposion and care for the handicapped resonated in both Greek and Jewish cultures.

40. *Reading Luke*, 224–25.

41. See Weinert's "The Meaning of the Temple in Luke-Acts," *BTB* 11 (1981) 89. Also consult his "Luke, the Temple, and Jesus' Saying about Jerusalem's Abandoned House (Luke 13:34–35)," *CBQ* 44 (1982) 68–76.

42. See Carolyn Gratton, *Trusting: Theory and Practice* (New York: Crossroad, 1982).

43. See S. Brown, *Apostasy and Perseverance*, for more detail

44. There is no space available here for a discussion of the Lukan theme of women. See Chapter Three above and its discussion of Luke 13:10–17.

Chapter Six

CONCLUSION

I would like to conclude this study of Luke, the artist and theologian, by reviewing, from fresh perspectives, the key elements of the foregoing chapters. In the first chapter I explained the notion of theme. I used "theme" as the means of exploring the theology of Luke because a thematic approach to a work of literature is familiar to both scholars and non-scholars. The writing of this book was not the place and the time for me to employ the literary theories of reader-response or structuralism.

It is my hope that the examination of the themes of the faithful God, food, and justice have shed considerable light on the much discussed question of why Luke places so little stress on Jesus' death as atonement for sin. It is my conviction that a continued probing of the Lukan themes will lead to insightful solutions to other Lukan problematics, e.g., the role of the Law.

Also in Chapter One I noted that God's purpose for creation and humankind is to be seen in the Lukan view of the Christ event, especially in God's vindication of Jesus. The disciples *see* God's purpose for life as the risen Jesus unfolds the meaning of God's scriptures for them (Luke 24:31–32,45–46). What they saw only incipiently at the cross (see Luke 23:49) is now made clear, and made clear at meals (see 24:13–35,41–48). Jesus once again shares God's life through the gift of food and thus makes known that God has vindicated him, his innocently suffering righteous one. God's purpose for creation and humankind is indeed life, and that purpose is seen in the life and vindication of Jesus, the righteous one and giver of food.

Chapters Two, Three, and Four are helpfully summarized under the theme of discipleship. As we saw from time to time above in our treatments of justice and food, the disciples are aligned with Jesus and share his life-style. They are not the religious leaders nor are they the people. When, like Judas, they move over to the life-style of the religious leaders, they equivalently abandon Jesus' journey and are no longer disciples.

The disciples are those who are given to know "the secrets of the kingdom of God" (Luke 8:10). The risen Jesus opens their eyes, which had previously not been able to perceive (Luke 9:45; 18:34), to see him as the rejected prophet (Luke 24), whose rejection by humankind does not spell an end to God's gracious action. In Jesus' name they are to proclaim forgiveness of sins to all nations (Luke 24:47–48). Their witness to the Christ event will not be one of word only, for their very lives will embody Jesus' life-style of justice and sharing food. In sum, the Lukan disciple is one who continues to body forth Jesus' vision of the faithful God.

In Chapter Five we viewed Jesus' death from the perspectives of the faithful God, justice, and food. Luke does see Jesus' death as salvific, but does so without using the thought world of separation from what is unclean, polluted, and enslaved. In Luke Jesus' life is not said to be given as a ranson from enslavement (contrast Mark 10:45), nor does his death effect a separation from the realm of the unclean. Rather the Lukan sotcriology accentuates the thought world of forgiveness of enemies, righteous sharing of life with the poor, eating and drinking together, actions which integrate rather than separate. The Lukan soteriology is with-ness, not separation. It is with consummate insight that scholars have called Luke 23:40–43 "The Gospel within the Gospel," for in many ways Lukan soteriology can be summarized in its verse 43: "Today you will be *with* me in paradise."

In Chapters One through Five I have purposely left "reader" somewhat vague in my text, when I asked, for example, "Can the reader believe in this God?" Through my vagueness I sought to involve contemporary believers in responding to the Lukan kerygmatic narrative. The faithful God, justice, and food are not themes which the passage of time has swept onto the dustpan of history. Modern-day innocently suffering righteous persons, and victims of unjust discrimination, and the millions who die each year from hunger in a world of bounty question the justice and faithfulness of God and God's believers. In this situation Luke's optimism is faith's life. In the Christ event God has shown that the food of life and not death is his will. In Jesus, the innocently suffering righteous one, God has shown that he is with those who suffer and die innocently for righteousness. Luke, the artist, breathes life into disciples, those weary travelers along justice's road, not by giving a detailed roadmap, but by projecting a vision. Can readers believe in the faithful God of Jesus, the righteous glutton and drunkard, who passionately longs to eat at table with them all?

SELECTED BIBLIOGRAPHY

This bibliography deals only with works in English and is not meant to include all the materials cited in the footnotes. It is a working bibliography for those who want to pursue the major themes developed in this book.

SURVEY OF RECENT LUKAN STUDIES

LaVerdiere, Eugene. "The Gospel of Luke: What the exegetes are saying about Luke's Gospel today," *The Bible Today* 18 (July, 1980) 226–35.

Richard, Earl. "Luke—Writer, Theologian, Historian: Research and Orientation of the 1970's," *Biblical Theology Bulletin* 13 (1983) 3–15.

General Orientation to Lukan Themes

Fitzmyer, Joseph A. *The Gospel According to Luke (I–IX): Introduction, Translation, and Notes.* Anchor Bible 28; Garden City; Doubleday, 1981, pp. 143–270.

Navone, John. *Themes of St. Luke.* Rome: Gregorian University Press, 1970.

THE CROSS

Crowe, Jerome. "The Laos at the Cross: Luke's Crucifixion Scene," *The Language of the Cross.* Ed. Aelred Lacomara; Chicago: Franciscan Herald, 1977, pp. 75–101.

Kodell, Jerome. "Luke's Theology of the Death of Jesus," *Sin, Salvation, and the Spirit: Commemorating the Fiftieth Year of The Liturgical Press.* Ed. Daniel Durken; Collegeville: Liturgical, 1979, pp. 221–30.

Tiede, David L. *Prophecy and History in Luke-Acts*. Philadelphia: Fortress, 1980, pp. 97–125. N.B. For a more complete bibliography, see Chapter Five above, note four.

FOOD

Dumm, Demetrius. "Luke 24:44–49 and Hospitality," *Sin, Salvation, and the Spirit: Commemorating the Fiftieth Year of The Liturgical Press*. Ed. Daniel Durken; Collegeville: Liturgical, 1979, pp. 231–39.

Feeley-Harnik, Gillian. *The Lord's Table: Eucharist and Passover in Early Christianity*. Symbol and Culture; Philadelphia: University of Pennsylvania, 1981, pp. 71–106.

Minear, Paul S. "Some Glimpses of Luke's Sacramental Theology," *Worship* 44 (1970) 322–31.

JUSTICE

Donahue, John R. "Biblical Perspectives on Justice," *The Faith That Does Justice: Examining the Christian Sources for Social Change*. Ed. J.C. Haughey; Woodstock Studies 2; New York: Paulist, 1977, pp. 68–112.

Guinan, Michael D. *Gospel Poverty: Witness to the Risen Christ, A Study in Biblical Spirituality*. New York: Paulist, 1981.

Perrin, Norman. *Jesus and the Language of the Kingdom: Symbol and Metaphor in New Testament Interpretation*. Philadelphia: Fortress, 1976, pp. 15–32.

Reumann, John. *"Righteousness" in the New Testament: "Justification" in the United States Lutheran-Roman Catholic Dialogue. With Responses by Joseph A. Fitzmyer and Jerome D. Quinn*. Philadelphia: Fortress; New York/Ramsey: Paulist, 1982, pp. 135–43 (#244–53).

POSSESSIONS, RICH, POOR

Johnson, Luke T. *Sharing Possessions: Mandate and Symbol of Faith*. Overtures to Biblical Theology; Philadelphia: Fortress, 1981.

Karris, Robert J. "Poor and Rich: The Lukan Sitz im Leben," *Perspectives on Luke-Acts*. Ed. Charles H. Talbert; Macon: Mercer University, 1978, pp. 112–25.

Schuessler Fiorenza, Elisabeth. *In Memory of Her: A Feminist Theological Reconstruction of Christian Origins*. New York: Crossroad, 1983, pp. 130–43.

Rejected Prophet

Dillon, Richard J. "Easter Revelation and Mission Program in Luke 24:46–48," *Sin, Salvation, and the Spirit: Commemorating the Fiftieth Year of The Liturgical Press*. Ed. Daniel Durken; Collegeville: Liturgical, 1979, pp. 240–70.

Tiede, David L. *Prophecy and History in Luke-Acts*. Philadelphia: Fortress, 1980, pp. 19–63.

INDEX OF BIBLICAL REFERENCES

INDEX OF AUTHORS

George, A., 116 n. 4
Gloeckner, R., 13 n. 18; 40 n. 6;
    116 n. 4
Gratton, C., 119 n. 42
Guinan, M.D., 32; 39 n. 3; 42 n.
    27; 124
Gutierrez, G., 46

Hands, A.R., 75 n. 45
Hanks, T., 46
Harrelson, W., 76 n. 60
Haulotte, E., 86
Hengel, M., 78 n. 69
Hoehner, H.W., 117 n. 11; 118 n.
    21

Iser, W., 11 n. 8
Isherwood, B., 71 n. 7

Jeremias, J., 58–59; 76 n. 54; 77
    n. 66; 102; 103
Johnson, L.T., 2 n. 1; 32; 39 n. 2
    and 3 and 4; 117 n. 10; 124

Karris, R.J., 2 n. 1; 3 n. 3 and 4;
    39 n. 5; 45; 125
Keck, L.E., 45
Kingsbury, J.D., 12 n. 13; 13 n.
    18
Klaiber, W., 44 n. 46
Kodell, J., 40 n. 6 and 10; 72 n.
    10; 116 n. 4; 123
Kurz, W.S., 14 n. 22

LaVerdiere, E., 43 n. 39; 72 n.
    11; 76 n. 58; 123

MacMallen, R., 74 n. 37
Mackey, J.P., 71 n. 2
Maddox, R., 117 n. 7
Malina, B.J., 45
Maly, E.H., 44 n. 41
Marshall, I.H., 2 n. 2; 41 n. 13
    and 16; 59; 73 n. 26; 74 n. 36
    75 n. 38; 86; 119 n. 38
Meeus, X. de, 75 n. 46
Merk, O., 43 n. 29
Merkel, H., 78 n. 69
Miller, J.H., 71 n. 5
Miller, P.D., 43 n. 38
Minear, P.S., 13 n. 19; 14 n. 24;
    40 n. 10; 67; 69; 71 n. 4; 124
Miranda, J.P., 73 n. 16

Navone, J., 3 n. 5; 10 n. 2; 44 n.
    41; 71 n. 4; 116 n. 3; 123
Neusner, J., 42 n. 24
Neyrey, J., 116 n. 4
Nickelsburg, G.W.E., 45; 117 n.
    6
Norris, F.W., 45
Nuetzel, J., 30; 44 n. 43

Oepke, A., 118 n. 21

Perrin, N., 30; 75 n. 39; 124
Peterson, N.R., 2 n. 1
Pilgrim, W., 32

Quasten, J., 86

Rasmussen, L.L., 45
Reumann, J., 38 n. 1; 40 n. 9; 42
    n. 27; 124